Into The Depths of My Mind

Short Stories Volume One

By B.E. Fidler

Trigger Warnings

Where the darkness lives, the demented spawns. From my biggest fears to the world's darkest secrets be forewarned of the vivid tales beyond this page that make the inky black of night shiver. Content may include death of main or sub-characters, imprisonment, rape, murder, and war. Also, the last story was previously published as part of an anthology and contains a female with multiple partner storyline.

CONTENTS

1 GRADUATION

Don't trip, chin up, smile, left foot, right foot, breathe, don't trip. Ignore the noise, don't look at the faces. They're not there; just tell yourself they are not there. Don't trip, chin up, smile, left foot, right foot, breathe, don't trip. This person is real; you must respond. Open your mouth and say thank you, shake the outstretched hand without flinching. Don't trip, hold on to what was given to you, chin up, smile, left foot, right foot, breathe, don't trip. Keep going, you're almost free. Don't trip, hold on to what was given to you, chin up, smile, left foot, right foot, breathe, don't trip. There is the exit; the people who are not there are definitely not watching the exit. Don't trip, chin up, smile, left foot, right foot, breathe, don't trip. You did it!

2 THE TERRORS OF NIGHT

I sat with my back pressed into the corner; sirens had sent me fleeing to this, my safe spot hidden from the world, and a resounding crack that had split the air so completely that I was sure the very fabric of existence would tear open, and my warriors of stuffed animals that encompassed me in their safety would be sucked into a pitch-black void. The kind of black void that resided in the eyes of the man with my mother. The man with the yellow-stained crooked teeth and bug bite-riddled face. The man from the shadows that only appears when daddy is at work, and I am supposed to be fast asleep in my room.

I shook my head, voices ricocheting down the hall and through my door. I froze, unwilling to dislodge my stuffed animal protectors even if it was to dispel that putrid memory of the man who I had woken up to sitting on my bed, cross-legged and silent, what felt like hours ago in this eternal night.

My mother had led him away, luring him away like a wild animal to some unknown treat that must have been horrifying and painful for her. Her screams had finally stopped, but no sooner had she quieted, had the noise of the cracking dimension drawn the sirens to our home.

My door opened, and I snapped my eyes closed as if my gleaming, tear-filled eyes would be a beacon to the trespasser entering my room.

"Ginny?" my father's voice cut through the terror ravaging my body.

I popped out of the animals as if sprouting wings. I sprung across the room and into his arms, his badge pinching my armpit, but the pain reminded me that I was awake and safe. The noise was numbing. The lights seemed too bright as I was carried out of my room and down the hall. I peeked over daddy's shoulder, catching sight of my mother, her body like a doll twisted across the coffee table, and a dark red cherry cordial covering her hair and the floor flashed by as I was whisked out the front door and past a shadowy figure in the yard that a flashlight passed over, sending shivers down my spine as yellow teeth flashed in the darkness before I was tucked into daddy's squad car.

3 I WENT QUICKLY

I slung my backpack over my shoulder, tightening the strap. Then, I unlatched the lock on the windowsill and glanced at the alarm connections. Earlier, I had pried them off the window and sill before the alarm was set and the screaming had started. Music was vibrating my bedroom floor, and the cops had already driven by once on a noise complaint.

I grasped the window and pushed it up. I tried to stay silent even though I had barricaded my door with my dresser, desk, and anything else I was strong enough to lift. I stuck my leg out the window, pausing to glance back at my bed. I had stuffed pillows under my blanket and stuck a kid's wig on my bear, setting him on my pillow. The wig had covered up my shaved scalp when my hair had been sheared off by the garbage disposal.

I felt myself begin to choke up with tears. The bear had to stay; I knew that I couldn't carry him, and he wouldn't fit in my backpack. I blew my bear a kiss and pulled myself out the window and onto the roof. I turned to pull the window closed, then turned to my planned path across the roof to the garage where I had seen the ladder leaning from fixing the kitchen light when the vodka bottle had smashed it.

I stepped lightly, my arms out to help me balance as I moved. The music blasted into the night, and I froze, kneeling and clamping my hands over my mouth. I heard yelling, then the crash of the trash can hitting the side gate. Then a slam from the back door, and the music was muffled. I removed my hand, and crawled the rest of the way, my legs shaking.

I reached the drop to the garage roof and listened for the sound of things breaking over the music. I turned, lowering my legs down. The roof scratched my stomach as I struggled to slide silently off the roof. I thudded to the roof of the garage, pressing myself against the house, knowing that the stairs were on the other side of this wall. I waited, listening, then scrambled to the other side on tiptoe, looking over the side for the ladder. I squinted in the darkness and slowly moved along the edge of the roof, looking for a glint of the metal.

I felt panic begin to set in; this was my last chance. I glanced out over the driveway, spotting the ladder in the back of the big, dirty gray truck parked in the driveway. I looked back the way I came to my window above, then turned back to the truck and stood up. I backed up, took a deep breath, clenched my fists, then ran, jumping off the side of the top of the garage roof. My shoe connected with the hood of the truck, and my hands shot out to brace my fall. The left windshield wiper cut into my hand, and my head bounced off the windshield. I rolled, falling off the truck to the unforgiving pavement on the driveway, my head spinning.

I scrambled up, holding my head. Then, realizing my feet were solid on the ground, I began to run. I didn't go toward the road.

I headed for the woods, their dark branches welcoming me to a safety that I had never known. I didn't slow to take it in. I ran, tripping and sprawling as I went. But each time, I pushed myself up off the ground and continued. The silence of the woods pressed in on me as my breath grew ragged, and my body began to shut down with exhaustion. I finally slowed but forced my aching legs to keep walking. I reached a large flat rock and had to stop, looking down at the drop beyond. I fell to my knees, tears brimming my eyes. I wasn't far enough, not nearly so. I couldn't go on; my whole body hurt. I couldn't stay here; I would be found by the dogs.

I looked up at the stars; they were beautiful, twinkling at me in the silence of the night. I turned to look for her constellation. I spotted it, moving to lean back on my arms. I teetered back, my hands never finding solid ground. My body fell back, the stars swirling around me as I fell, the air cold, the stars everywhere, then blackness. What I would have given to have my bear.

4 CASTLE PEAK

We waited for weeks, counting down day by day. Finally, when the day came, I woke up to my alarm, shooting straight up in bed, excitement filling me. I looked at the calendar on the wall and cheered with delight, springing out of bed. I stumbled as my foot caught on the blanket. I steadied myself, then snatched my clothes from atop my dresser. I rushed to the bathroom down the hall.

"No! I get to use it first," my little brother called as I closed and locked the door.

I ignored the pounding on the door as I showered quickly, then dressed, brushed my teeth, and untangled my wet black hair.

"Avery, I am going to use your trash can as a toilet if you don't hurry up," my little brother yelled from outside the door.

I opened the door, "Collin, what are you waiting for?" I teased, passing him.

He whined, running into the bathroom, and slamming the door behind him. I went downstairs, the scent of bacon wafting through the air. I skipped into the kitchen and hopped onto a stool, grasping the counter as the stool teetered to the side.

"Good morning, Avery. Dare I ask if you're ready to go?" my mother asked as she set three pieces of bacon on my plate and flopped one pancake down as well. She slid the plate over. I had a hot piece of bacon off the plate and in my mouth before the plate stopped before me.

"Yes…" I murmured, my mouth full of bacon. My mother scowled, her green eyes—a duplicate pair of my own—giving me a piercing stare as she plated food for my brother as he shuffled in, glaring at me. I ignored him, shoving a big bite of pancake into my mouth.

"Avery, you're going to choke," my mother chastised. My father came in from the garage, and I chewed faster.

"Good morning, Collin," he greeted, kissing my brother on the top of his head. "Morning, Avery. Is my camping girl almost ready to go?" he asked, tugging playfully on my hair.

"Yes, Dad," I managed to say before devouring my last bite of pancake.

"When will Eden be here?" he asked, stealing bacon off Collin's plate. The doorbell rang, and I laughed, jumping down and dodging around my dad. I shot toward the front door. I pulled the door open, and Eden stood with her backpack slung over her shoulder and her sleeping bag under her arm.

"Bye, Dad," she yelled over her shoulder.

"Sunscreen," he called back and then drove off as we waved goodbye. I grabbed Eden's hand and tugged her inside.

"Let's go, let's go," I chanted, sliding my feet into my shoes and kneeling to tie them.

"Hello, Eden. Would you like some breakfast?" my mother asked.

"No, we need to leave," I blurted.

"Avery Jean Lambert, you will not be rude," my mom lectured.

"Yes, mom. Sorry, Eden," I said, standing up.

"No, thank you, Mrs. Lambert. My mom stuffed me like a turkey this morning," Eden said, rubbing her stomach.

My mom laughed and went back to the kitchen. "Good thing we aren't going hunting," Dad jokes, taking Eden's sleeping bag.

"Ewe…" She and I said at the same time, then started giggling. I loved our twin moments; they were far and few between. We are the same height, but the similarities end there. I, for one, am ghost pale, and Eden never needs to tan. Her eyes are a deep chocolate brown, beautiful and nothing like mine.

"What are you two slowpokes doing? Say bye to Mom and Collin, let's go," Dad urged, grinning as he dashed out the garage door. We shrieked, racing after him. I yanked at the doorknob, but it didn't budge. "Say bye to Mom and Collin," my dad bellowed through the door.

I groaned, then went to the kitchen. "Bye, Mom," I said and hugged her, snatching a piece of bacon behind her back. I winked at Collin, then ripped the bacon in half, handing him some as I ruffled his hair. "Bye, Collin," I said, walking back to the door to the garage where Eden stood and waited.

"Goodbye, Mrs. Lambert. Bye, Collin," she called toward the kitchen.

"Be good," Mom called back. I grabbed the handle, twisted hard, and threw my shoulder into the door. To my surprise, Dad wasn't holding it anymore, and I toppled out onto the floor of the garage. The Cherokee roared to life as Eden put her hand down to help me up. I grabbed it, both of us laughing as I heaved myself up off the floor. We got into the Cherokee and buckled up.

"Okay, ladies, the rules," dad announced.

We groaned but waited for him to continue.

"We stay belted at all times while the vehicle is running, we stay together, and follow my directions at all times," he explained, staring at us in the rearview mirror. "Oh, and I get to choose the tunes," he added, grasping the steering wheel in one hand and putting the car in drive with the other.

"No!" We cried as he laughed mechanically, driving down the driveway. I looked back at our house just as Collin burst out the front door to wave at us as we rolled away. Dad honked the horn as we turned the corner at the end of the street and then headed for the interstate.

"How long will it take to get there?" I asked curiously biting my lip and sitting back.

"Castle Peak is about three hours away," Dad explained pointing out the window in the general direction.

"Don't you need the GPS that mom stuck in here?" I asked pulling it from a cupholder.

"I don't need a GPS. I am a mental map," he swore, merging onto the interstate. He turned up Eden's and my favorite station, and we all began to sing Eden and I dancing in the back seat. This was our first time camping, and we were ready.

About an hour into our adventure, Dad left the interstate and headed for the mountains. He pulled into a gas station a few minutes later and parked next to a pump, glancing at us in the mirror to make sure we hadn't unbuckled yet. He smiled as our hands hovered over the buckles. He turned off the Cherokee, and we unbuckled, hopping out and stretching. "Bathroom snacks, go," Dad said, and we rushed towards the building.

The door was heavy and took all my strength to get it open so we could scurry in as Dad pumped gas. I grabbed Eden's hand, and we snaked our way through the aisles to the back where a huge old neon sign read "washrooms." We found the ladies' room and rushed in to take care of business. I glanced in the mirror as I washed my hands and then glanced over at Eden's reflection, wishing my hair could be so wavy and beautiful. But my hair was straight and flat. I dried my hands, nudging Eden as I walked past.

"I can't wait to get there," she said, following me.

"I know, our tent is so cool," I added, leading her back to the main part of the store. "What kind of snack do you want?" I asked, looking around.

She shrugged. My best friend was a girl of few words most of the time, but the silence was so comfortable and helped me stay calm.

"Salty, sweet, crunchy—oh, I know, venison beef jerky," I said, pointing out the bag and sticking my tongue out in disgust.

"You are crazy," Eden said, walking further down an aisle. I looked toward the door, watching my dad head towards us. "Something that won't melt," Eden suggested, walking past the chocolate.

I pouted but followed her over to the trail mix she was now examining. "Banana chips and dried pineapple?" she asked, pulling them off the shelf. I made a face. "They taste great, I promise," she added.

I shrugged, "Okay," I agreed. I had to trust her on healthy food. Her mom was a huge health nut. I wasn't allowed to repeat those words to her by penalty of being grounded for life by my mom.

We walked toward my dad, who raised an eyebrow but smiled. "Grab some juice or water as well," he urged, snagging a pack of sunflower seeds off a shelf and handing them to me along with a twenty-dollar bill. "Be right out," he called over as he headed to the washroom sign. We went to the checkout and set our items on the counter, grabbing water from a cooler next to it.

"Will this be all for you ladies today?" a woman asked. Her name tag read "Michelle," and her shirt had a picture of a moose on it.

"Yes, please," I replied, smiling politely, still looking at the moose as she began to scan everything.

"That will be $11.65 today," Michelle announced, setting our things in a bag. I slid the twenty over to her, then glanced back toward the washroom sign to look for dad. "Aren't you two a bit young to be wandering around alone?" she asked, handing me change.

"We are 15," I argued.

"Our parents trust us," Eden assured standing up straighter.

"Trusting you two isn't what I am worried about," Michelle said, watching a man walk past us. We glanced at each other, and I grabbed our bag.

"Thank you," I called, pulling Eden out the door. We rushed to the car, not looking back. I opened the door, and we both got in. I reached over to Dad's seat and locked the doors. Eden looked at me and then looked out the windows, no one was nearby, but the woman's words seemed to hang low over our heads.

"Do you think she was just messing with us?" I asked Eden nervousness tensing her body.

"You don't want to hear the statistics of her being correct," Eden responded, staring at the door, seemingly trying to will my dad to walk out. He did pop out a few excruciating minutes later. A huge grin on his face as he walked over and reached to open the driver's side door only to find it locked. I sprung over the seat, unlocked it, and then sat back in my seat, buckling up.

"Everything okay?" Dad asked, looking back at us.

"Sure," I said, dismissing his worried glance.

"Okay, time to roll out," my dad announced, chuckling at his joke as he started the Cherokee. I glanced over to check that Eden was buckled and then felt silly for checking; Eden always followed the rules. I was the one who typically toed the line. We drove on for a good thirty minutes until Dad slowed and pulled to the side of the road, looking at a split in the road.

"How's your mental map going?" I asked, hiding my smile.

"Shush," he said, pulling back onto the street and turning right. He sped up as we approached a side hill. A sign ahead caught my attention. I squinted, trying to read it. "Castle Peak 30 miles ahead," Dad read, pointing out the sign.

The Cherokee jerked to the right. I tried to grab the seat to hold on, but the Cherokee seemed to buck, and the next thing I knew, I was upside down, pressure on my lap as I hung upside down, a scream bursting from my lips. I stared ahead as things seemed to fall around me. I saw the pineapples as if in slow motion hit the ceiling below me, and I felt the change in my pocket shifting, a few coins falling free from my pocket as I wiggled in shock.

"Dad?" I asked, fear engulfing me. I looked toward Eden, who hung next to me, her arms hanging down toward the ceiling, unmoving. I looked around, seeing all the camping gear spewed out below us. I reached for my belt, my head hurting from hanging upside down. I unbuckled slowly, with one hand reaching down to the ceiling so I wouldn't fall on my head. I collapsed in a heap and then sat up, looking around toward Eden and Dad. I looked toward Eden's window; red caught my eye. Blood smeared the glass. I froze for a second, then jolted forward. "Eden!" I screamed. "Daddy, Eden is hurt!" I cried, reaching for him. I froze momentarily as I saw blood dripping onto the ceiling. "Daddy!" I screamed, feeling the broken glass cut at my palms as I crawled toward him. He groaned, and I sighed in relief, turning back to Eden. From where I now crouched between the two front seats, I could see Eden's window, which was unbroken and smeared with blood.

I yanked her sleeping bag out of the bramble of stuff next to me and put it under her. I rested her head on my shoulder and carefully reached up and unlatched her belt. She fell on me and the sleeping bag with an audible cry. I grabbed her sleeping bag and yanked it towards my open smashed window.

She felt like she weighed 100 pounds as I struggled through the glass to pull her free from the wreckage. I stared at the blood seeping from beneath her brown locks of hair, then looked around toward the sign up the hill, then looked back at the Cherokee and crawled over, not feeling as though I had the strength to stand. My body was shaking, and the mud beneath my hands squelched over my fingers as I went.

I crawled back into my window and into the front passenger seat. "Daddy, wake up," I demanded, shaking his shoulder slightly. He groaned, and his eyes fluttered open. He looked confused, then his arms shot out, and he yelled incoherently. "Daddy, you need to unbuckle; we need to get out of here," I begged. He stared at me, reaching to me and caressing my face. "Come on," I urged, "Eden needs you," I explained. His eyes widened, and he reached down to the ceiling.

"Unbuckle me, Avery," he grunted. I reached up, undoing his belt and moving as he collapsed on the ceiling, looking around in fear. His nose was bleeding freely and looked crooked.

"She's outside," I said, leading the way. Dad followed me out and over to where Eden lay.

"My phone is in the glove box; we need to get it and call 911," he ordered. I didn't hesitate. I crawled back over and into the front. I tried to open the glove box, but it would not budge. I looked over, saw Dad's keys hanging out of the ignition, and pulled them free, trying the key on the lock. The box clattered open, everything falling out at my knees. I grabbed his phone and headed back to him. I handed him the phone, and he looked at it for a moment, his other hand holding his head as a pained look appeared on his face. He then called 911.

"Hello? Yes, this is Jack Lambert. We just rolled our vehicle near Castle Peak, about 30 miles down the mountain; a little girl is unconscious. There was a dog in the road, and I swerved; it's all my fault," Dad choked out, tears streaming down his face. I stared; I had never seen my dad cry.

I looked back at the Cherokee. Crawling over, I searched but couldn't find the first aid kit. So, I crawled back to my dad. He was fussing over Eden, but I couldn't look at her. What if she was dead? My brain screamed. I struggled to my feet, looking around. "Stay close, be careful, are you hurt?" My dad called after me. I ignored him, looking around. I spotted movement ahead and walked forward, stumbling slightly. A dog sat shaking near the road, staring at me as I approached.

"Come here, boy," I called, reaching a hand out to him. I then noticed my hand shaking and the blood crusted on my hands, and I sat down, overwhelmed. My eyes locked on my hands, knowing the blood was Eden's. The dog whimpered and crawled into my lap, nuzzling my face, and licking my dirty, blood-ridden hands. I got back up, clutching the dog to me as I went back to Eden. I sat back down. The dog sniffed Eden, licking her face. I looked up at my dad, but his hands covered his face as he cried.

"Ewe," I heard Eden moan. I looked down as her arm reached for the dog.

My dad looked down and began to sob louder. "Oh, thank you, Lord," he cried.

As we waited for the paramedics, a large black truck rumbled up the road, stopping with a screech from its brakes and then a loud groan from the emergency brake just before the engine died out. I heard a door slam, and then the man from the market appeared around the truck. He had a first aid kit tucked under his arm as he jogged to us. His belly bouncing and his beard feathered out as he hoofed down the hill.

My heart raced as the woman's words hit me like a ton of bricks. The man fell to his knees next to my father, whose eyes were swelling closed. "You okay, mister?" the burly man asked.

"No," my father grumbled, and I stared at him, a fresh wave of fear washing over me. I couldn't stop staring until Eden reached out and took my hand. I looked down at her, tears filling my eyes as they fell upon my best friend.

I took a deep breath, then looked back up, but the man was no longer next to my father. I looked back towards his truck to see him yanking things from the back. I patted Eden's arm. "Can I help?" I called, getting shakily to my feet.

The man looked up as he made his way down the hill and gave me a whiskery smile. His eyes seemed kind, and some of my fear faded. "Do you have any more sleeping bags, sweetheart?" he asked.

I nodded slightly and went over to the Cherokee. Kneeling and peeking inside, I spotted Dad's tightly rolled pack lying in the shamble of supplies and crawled in to get it. I popped back out and walked over and handed it to the man.

"Thank you," he said and swiftly unrolled it and laid it on the ground behind Dad. "Okay, mister, do you think you can manage to make it onto the sleeping bag?" he asked. My dad didn't respond but moved onto the sleeping bag. "Good, now lay back," the man urged, and my dad did so with no hesitation.

"His name is Jack," I said, my voice sounding small and alien to my ears.

The man looked up. "My name is Tom Grady. It's nice to meet you, Jack," he said as he wrapped a blanket around my dad.

"My name is Avery," I added, sitting down next to Eden. "And this is Eden," I continued, the nerves making me chatty.

"It's good to see you both again. I think we passed Michelle's store earlier," he recalled. I could see Eden's hands clutch the dog a little closer, but I nodded in agreement.

"You must have a good memory," my father praised with a half-smile.

"Actually, Miss Avery here looks a lot like my little girl Beth who passed away a few years back," Mr. Grady explained sadness pulling at his mouth.

"Sorry to hear that," my father said, his breathing evening out as he looked like he was about to fall asleep.

"No sleeping, sorry Jack," Mr. Grady urged. "I heard the paramedics on my CB in the truck; they're not too far," he assured, patting my dad's hand.

We sat in silence for what seemed like forever until the paramedics pulled up, and dad and Eden were loaded side by side into the ambulance. I rode in the police car alone, shivering as I held the dog to me. Mr. Grady followed us to the nearest hospital so he could give his statement to the police and see how everyone was doing.

Dad's nose was broken, and he had a good bump on his head. However, Eden had a severe concussion and bruises from the seatbelt. We clutched that dog in our arms until we were sent home. We never did make it up to Castle Peak, and Eden's parents didn't let her come over much anymore. Her parents blamed my dad just as he blamed himself. There was no longer any trust between our dads, only hostility, but I got to go to her house to visit her dog, Castle, as often as I wanted. I was always welcome. At first, they kept thanking me and telling me I was a hero, but I finally convinced them to stop and reminded them when the subject arose that Eden would have done the same if the roles had been reversed.

My dad did reach out to Mr. Grady. He comes to our house for Thanksgiving every year. We learned that first Thanksgiving when Dad offered Mr. Grady a glass of wine that his family had died in a car crash and that he had been driving and had had just one too many when their vehicle had hit ice and flown off the road. Unlike our crash, they rolled several times, and unlike our rules, little Beth was not seat-belted in the back of the car. We were his new family now, a substitute for the one he couldn't save years ago.

5 ALONE IN THE WOODS

It was dark and chilly in the tent. Gracie shifted in her sleep, trying to find a comfortable position on the solid, stone-riddled ground. A snap of a branch made Gracie's eyelids pop open. Her steel gray eyes stared at the wall of her tent unseeingly as she listened intently. She scowled silently, mentally berating herself for being scared. This camping trip had been Gracie's idea; she had planned it out for months. She had found a location, invited a few friends, and saved one hundred and twenty-five dollars to pay for her equipment and travel expenses. She closed her eyes, not letting the disappointment of the nearly canceled trip ruin her plans.

As she began to drift into a much-needed slumber, there was a rustle from outside her tent. She sat up this time, clutching her lavender sleeping bag to her. Her eyes tried to search for her flashlight as the rustling continued.

"Ouch," she heard someone whisper.

She gulped, her throat drying like the deserts of Nevada. Her hand released the sleeping bag, fumbling for the flashlight. Why had she come alone? her brain chastised. She had lied to her father that the others were meeting her out here. But in truth, everyone had bailed, all for some idiotic movie being released. The darkness seemed to press down around her as her hand frantically searched and then found the flashlight. The cold metal greeted her fingers with an ambiance of safety. She racked her brain, squelching the fear back as she decided what she should do.

A loud crash reverberated around Gracie as her tent shook violently. She flinched then raised her chin, refusing to cower. She was brave, she silently reminded herself. She shimmied out of her sleeping bag, reaching for the zipper to the tent as she clutched her flashlight to her. Gracie unzipped the tent, stepped out, and clicked her flashlight on. In a thunderous voice, she yelled, "What the hell are you doing here?" Her words were like venom dripping from her lips, causing the teenage boy standing in the beam of her flashlight to plow over her camping chair.

With a resounding thud, he crashed to the ground. "Sorry, I got lost," the boy cried, his sneakers scraping against the ground and his hands flailing to help himself back to his feet. "Sorry," he said, his eyes like two shining saucers in the light.

"Who are you?" Gracie asked sternly, her voice still cutting through the cold night air like a missile.

"Colt, my name is Colt," he informed his hands up in surrender.

Gracie moved forward, her light catching the shimmer of the violent rose-red of blood seeping from Colt's knee. "You're hurt," Gracie pointed out, her voice normal now.

Colt looked down. "Crap," he groaned.

"Sit down, I have a first aid kit," Gracie informs ducking back into her tent. She moves her journal from her bag as she rifles for her kit. Suddenly a large cold callused hand grasps her leg and yanks. Gracie screams, her throat retching in pain, the flashlight soaring from her hand as she clutches at her surroundings. The lavender sleeping bag slides like silk from her hands as another callused hand grabs her other ankle. She kicks and struggles but is dragged backward out of her tent. She prays that this is some kind of prank that her friends will pop out of the woods laughing at any moment. Rocks scrape her stomach as her shirt rides up under her armpits, her hands still trying to clutch onto something solid.

"Colt move your ass," A gravelly voice ordered. Gracie's legs were released, and she nosedived into the ground. Her bare feet tore at the ground trying to gain traction as she pushed herself up partially dazed, her nose bleeding. She just passed the back of her tent trying to burst out into a sprint when two hairy arms snatched her around the middle.

"Not so fast," A booming voice growled in her ear. A man spun her around and slammed her back against a tree one hand holding her hands together and the other clutching her neck pinning her to the tree. "Should have stayed in the tent," he spat his eyes raking over her. Gracie gasped, squirming tears streaming down her face. "Tank, what do you think?" the man asked, calling over his shoulder towards Colt and Tank as they approached.

Gracie's eyes bulged skirting from face to face then locking on Colt's a look of dismay plastered there in the dim light of the two older men's headlamps.

"Hold her still Rod," Tank suggested moving closer to Gracie, Rod's hand loosened slightly as Gracie's eyes began to roll back. She took a deep breath in and began to cough as she choked on the blood from her nose. Tank grabbed the front of Gracie's dusty shirt and yanked it up whipping at her face to remove the blood. He then grasped her breast squeezing it as though attempting to burst it. Gracie screamed then choked back as Tank's stubbly red-haired face jutted forward, his eyes locked on hers. "She will do just fine won't she Colt," Tank growled.

Gracie tried to look at Colt but couldn't see around Tank. She whimpered trying to think. "Let's take her back, Colt, clean up here, and we will have her ready for you," Rod decided, pulling a headlamp from his pocket and flinging it at Colt who flinched, barely catching it.

"No!" Gracie screamed bucking to the right trying feverishly to break free.

Tank grabbed her by the back of her pants, yanking her back to him he slid his hand down the back of her pants.

"Help!" Gracie belted. He grabbed her underwear and yanked it up as hard as she could. Gracie screamed in pain as her underwear ripped as it tore up into her. Rod pulled the underwear free holding Gracie to him with one arm.

"Shut up," Tank demanded as Colt scurried to clean up the disturbance at the campsite. Rod stuck Gracie's underwear in her mouth.

"You're only going to make it worse," Rod hissed in her ear. Gracie struggled for a moment as Tank walked in front of her. She took the best opportunity she had and kicked out hard. For a brief heart-wrenching moment Gracie was free no one had a hold on her, but in the next second, she was flung at the tree, her head connecting with the bark with a loud thud.

Gracie was unconscious as Rod lugged her up onto his shoulder and headed away from her camp followed closely by Tank. They had walked for an hour before they reached a house deep in the woods that was boarded over and covered in foliage. They walked through a decrepit room to a door that led down to the basement.

Colt took his time as he walked back, he had made the campsite look entirely undisturbed as he had been taught. But this was nothing like what his brothers had told him. They had always said that the bitches always had it coming, but this girl seemed momentarily sweet when she offered to fix up his knee. How did she deserve what his brothers were doing to her? He had to man up. He reminded himself what would happen if he didn't do what he was told to do. He shivered then paused, reaching the house. He could leave right now. They would be busy with her for hours. He moved forward, he didn't dare try to run and hated himself for considering it, family first always.

"Colt, it's about time," Tank called as the stairs squeaked under Colt's shoes as he descended. Gracie lay on the floor in a heap of completely naked blood smeared over her pale skin twitching.

"She's all ready for you kiddo," Rod offered.

Colt swallowed hard, nodding once his face like stone as he stared at her. His brothers clapped him on his back as they headed upstairs laughing and talking together. Colt's eyes were glued to Gracie's back. He moved forward unbuckling his belt he knelt down rolling her slowly to her back her eyes gleamed in the lamplight.

"Please," Gracie choked out.

Colt gave her a small nod leaning over her. He grasps her neck squeezing with all his strength her nails drag across his arm in a feeble attempt to stop him, till they fall and she lies limp and lifeless beneath him.

6 FALLEN ANGEL

I felt frozen. I could never remember ever being this cold, not ever. It ran deep; it felt as though the cold had penetrated and numbed my whole body down to the bone. I wanted to grab my warmest blanket, the dark green one with the frayed edge from getting stuck in the dryer. But my arms were too heavy. They must be frozen solid, I wonder. I opened my eyes to blackness; my left eye felt too tired and sluggish to open fully. How cold was it? I thought, horrified. I took a deep breath, trying to calm down, and let it out in a painful blow. The pain burned in my throat, but I was too distracted by the lack of condensation escaping me. Even in darkness, I should have felt the frigid air that must be making me so cold fill my lungs, but the air I drag into my lungs is warm and moist. The smell of soil filling my nostrils as panic begins to bloom in my chest.

Blinding light spiders webbed across the blackness above me, followed by an earthshaking rumble of thunder. I felt water splatter on my lips. I opened my mouth eagerly, praying the water would moisten my burning throat. I coughed as the rain began to pound down on me. I closed my mouth and used all my focus to turn my head away from the onslaught of rain surely drenching me. I gasped for air, now trying to not breathe in the water. I felt mud against my cheek and focused on the alien sensation. Anything but the dead cold feeling that riddled my body. As lightning lit up the heavens again, I risked a lookup, still unable to raise my head. Silhouettes blocked my view of the sky now that my head was tilted to the side. I felt my heart hammer in my chest, the noise of its frantic pulsing battling with the sound of thunder and rain. I waited for the next streak of lightning; this time determined to discover what was so close to me that it blocked my line of sight. The lightning crackled as if the heavens were breaking above me, lighting the rows of corn stalks impeding my vision.

My mind reeled. Corn stalks? There were no corn stalks in town limits. Why would I be this far from home? Wake up, Abigail, I thought wildly, hoping that the lack of sensation was merely a night terror, the pain in my throat from calling out in my fitful sleep. A prickling sensation began to cut into my left leg like the time my mother had used a scouring pad to rid my face of makeup when she had found me and my friend Violet playing in Violet's fort at the back corner of her property.

"Mother," I croaked. The prickling sensation began to spread like venom up and down my leg relentlessly. I screamed, my mouth quickly filling with dirty water. It was now that I realized the ground below me was no longer pressed firmly to my cheek. The mud had thinned as the downpour had begun to pool around me, the water rising. I spat the water out, coughing. I needed to get up, my brain demanded. I willed myself to move, to rise from the ground. I felt my finger twitch as finally, I gradually grasped at the muddy slush of water creeping higher around me. Relief flooded me for half a heartbeat before the prickling sensation ravaging my legs shot through my arms.

I blew out air, fighting to keep the filthy water from invading my mouth again. I focused on trying to turn my head back toward the sky; the rain coming down was more inviting than the disgusting water lapping at my mouth, hell-bent on releasing my soul into its gritty darkness. When I finally got my face pointed back to the sky, my whole body felt as if I was being shocked by the sound of thunder dulled by the water now covering my ears. My heartbeat was the only thing I could focus on as I writhed with pain. Praying hadn't helped. I had to figure out how to get up or I might as well give up and release my soul to the hungry storm above me. Lightning lit up the world around me, and I realized that the ground beneath the stalks to my right while wet-looking, was not flooded with water like the ground around and beneath me.

I screamed defiance and pain into the storm, my arm rising from the water just visible as light escaped back into the looming relentless clouds. I reached for the corn stalks; my body erased from the prickling as my limbs finally began to respond to my urgent brain. I felt the water swish away, the stalk's rough stem crushing against my palm, and I fell hard onto my stomach like a beached whale. Air escaped my body, my face smacking into the mud. I pushed against the ground as hard as I could. I opened my mouth, gasping for clean air, spitting out dirt and tiny rocks that tried to invade my mouth. I felt the water on my legs and reached back to cup some, trying feverishly to splash it on my face.

My left eye was still refusing to open completely. I gasped for air, trying to calm my racing heart. Thunder roared overhead, and the idea of being safe vanished from my mind. The storm wasn't letting up. I needed to find help. I gritted my teeth and screamed my throat raw as I made my body move. I began to crawl, knowing that crawling further into the corn would mean certain death, but the rising water would hold no better fate for me. So by the light of the intermittent lightning, I began to crawl. I wasn't sure what direction I was heading or how long my body would support me, but I had two choices: keep moving or succumb.

While at this moment it didn't seem as if God's will was for me to survive, I knew giving up was just as dishonorable as suicide. I would need to die fighting to live if I wanted to make it into the ranks of God's angels. I must have crawled for hours; after two failed attempts to rise to my feet were thwarted by pain that burned on my thighs, across my chest, my wrists, and deep within me at my core. This pain, while dull, was the scariest; there was no reason on this planet that I should hurt in my core. At some point, my arms gave out on me, and I collapsed face-first into soggy grass. My brain raced, even as my eyes closed, as the darkness pulled me into unconsciousness.

Bright, blinding light greeted me as my right eye opened again. This time, I had no false hope that heaven was greeting me;

the pain was too raw to present. I was horrified at my thoughts, wishing for the numb coldness back. A loud noise caught my attention, and I shifted painfully, the green grass tickling my nose. A large black lab bounded towards me, and I flinched, slamming my eyes closed, waiting for its big, white, sharp canines to pierce my skin. My eyes snapped back open when the dog's wet tongue began to lick my face. He howled into the air like a foghorn. I heard a whistle in the distance and reached for the massive dog, my hand nearly caressing his black fur before he tore away toward the direction of the whistle.

"No!" I gasped, trying to crawl after it. My arms refused to hold my weight. I looked at my arm stretched out next to me in anger. But the anger soon turned into shock as I realized that my mud-encrusted skin was not sheathed in clothes. I looked at my other arm, and it was also bare of modesty. I heard a voice and the dog barking, but instead of trying to track the voice with my eyes, I stared at my bare shoulder, stunned.

"Come on, boy, we have to get back to the house," a voice spoke from somewhere ahead of me. I tilted my head, looking toward the voice, my eyes locking onto the back of a man who was trying to lead the lab back the way he had come.

"Please," I tried to scream, but it came out as a whine. The dog shot back over to me, his tongue assaulting my face.

"Hunter, here boy, what do you have there, boy?" the man asked. I heard him gasp, then felt his hand pushing hair from my face as he scrambled onto the ground, pushing the dog away from me. "What the hell? Are you okay?" he asked, looking into my eyes, his face painted with worry. I opened my mouth to say no, but the world spun as he lifted me into the air. I was flush up against the plaid-covered chest of a man I had never met, his chocolate brown eyes and black shaggy hair looming above me, his strong arms cradling me like a baby. "Don't worry, you're safe. Hunter, come, we need to get her to the hospital," the man spoke. I felt like a rag doll being set into the front of his truck, his eyes looking different now as if the sight of me made his face shatter. He yanked a blanket from his back seat and tucked it around me, belting me in securely. I stared out the window of the truck at the lab sitting on the porch of an old farmhouse with green trim and a matching door.

I was pulled back into the blackness of my unconsciousness as corn flew past my window and the man's truck tore up the road toward where I hoped a hospital would sit.

Next time I woke I would spend weeks wishing to be back in the heart of the storm, or dead in a shallow grave off the side of a cornfield. When I woke up, I was not only disowned by my mother and father but also rejected by my church and alienated from the people I had mistakenly thought of as friends. It was not because they wished me dead, that they looked down on me for being in the hospital with a fracture to my left eye socket, bruising covering more than 50 percent of my body, lacerations to my right thigh, and various scratches and penetrations to my skin that would keep me bedridden for a time, until the realization of what had happened to me that terrible night.

I, once the heart of my church choir, was a solid B student who followed most rules and had volunteered all my time to my family's faith. Had been deflowered at 17 and left for dead off a dirt road near a cornfield. I was not a strong survivor. I had become a sinner; I had become a pariah. No one in my small town would look me in the eyes, even as my doctor explained to me that they had figured it out. He never used the word that shredded my soul. Raped and almost murdered. Me. Who was I? my brain questioned. The feelings that pressed in on me were not those of fear or uncertainty, but at first, were ones of shame, then anger.

When I was eventually released from the hospital, I was wheeled to the exterior doors where I was met by the sheriff's old cruiser. He had been one of the only people to question me and investigate what had happened. While I had no idea who had raped me, I was very sure of one thing: I needed to be out of this town. Out of the suffocating reminder that this place I had once treasured was now a dome of depression reminding me of everything I had lost, at no fault of my own.

I stayed at the sheriff's office long enough to figure out my plan and to pen a note to Hunter, the dog, and his heroic owner in their white farmhouse with green trim. I left the letter on the sheriff's desk as he spoke with family services. I dragged the small suitcase that my parents had supplied to the sheriff in an attempt to avoid me at all costs. I slipped silently out of the sheriff's office and out onto the street, my eyes down. I beelined toward the bus station. I felt eyes on me as I passed the market, the bookstore, and the church. When I reached the bus station, I pulled out the crumpled 20-dollar bills that I had liberated from the seam of the back of an old doll my mother had mercifully packed with my ID, birth certificate, toiletries, and a few outfits she had not burned with the rest of my belongings.

"One ticket to the city," I requested, not making eye contact with the old woman selling tickets. I felt her judgment as she slammed down her stamp on a ticket. She took my money, silently flinging back my change as if handing it to me would soil her good name.

I only waited 15 minutes for the bus, but it felt like an eternity on that bench in full view of all the judgmental and God-fearing members of my town that passed by; their eyes felt like lasers. It would be months before I found the courage to make eye contact with someone again. That person ended up being my First Sergeant in the United States Air Force at my commencement ceremony after completing basic training.

"How does it feel to be an official Airman?" he asked, his hand roughly thumping my shoulders.

"Freeing, sir," I responded, his eyes a green that spoke volumes of the things he had seen in his long life and career in the military.

He chuckled in response, and I smiled for the first time since before the storm. It would be years before I let myself think back to before I was enlisted. Years before the walls I had built up around me would come teetering down in a colossal mind-melting fiasco. I sat in front of my commanding officer, my back straight, my face impassive.

"Abigail," he began.

I flinched, recovering to my look of indifference quickly. "I have some unfortunate news," he continued, watching me for a moment. "We have been contacted by a lawyer from a town called Samsonton, in Illinois," he explained.

This time, I felt my jaw loosen as I listened intently, refusing to let the memories resurface.

"I am so sorry, Abigail, but it has come to our attention that your mother and father have both perished in a car accident. Their lawyer is requesting your attendance to settle their estate," he concluded. I stared at him transfixed. I should feel sad, my brain reminded me, but I could not pull that emotion into my heart. Confusion dimmed my senses slightly.

"There must be some mistake, sir," I argued shaking my head.

He held out a photo that he had printed from his computer, a picture of a picture. It was our old house in Samsonton, my parents standing side by side, respectfully not touching. I stood before them, young but unmistakable, my brown hair tamed by a ribbon on my head. I took the picture, ready to deny the request. Images flooded my mind as a memory forced its way into my consciousness. It was growing dark, and storm clouds were riding the horizon. The clicking of my shoes battled the songs of the crickets, and I walked down the sidewalk, my house coming into view down the road, lit by the light of beaming streetlights. A song I was humming moved like smoke through my brain. The serenity of the moment crumbled as I felt hands grab me around the middle, dragging me off the sidewalk and into a park.

"Abigail, are you okay? We have scheduled some time off for you; take as much time as you need," my commanding officer's voice broke through the memory. I looked down at my hands that were clutching the side of his desk, and I cleared my throat, shaking my head slightly and rising to my feet to gain my composure.

"Yes, sir," I said and saluted before leaving the office. I rented a car and drove back to Samsonton, back to the monsters of my past, back to discover the truth. I was strong now, I was brave. No one could control me with their judgment anymore. Dread set in the closer and closer I got to town. But as I parked outside the law office of Richie Douglas, I found that no eyes swept my way; it had been nearly ten years. No one recognized me; no one gave me a second thought. It was a treat to be invisible in this toxic town, if only for a while.

Richie wasn't in when I arrived, but in true small-town fashion, an envelope graced with my surname sat waiting for me with his secretary, who had no idea who I was. She must be new to town because her face didn't register to me either. Inside, the envelope held the keys to my childhood home and paperwork that explained that my parents had no will and everything was to go to the last remaining member of their family. Which happened to be me. This made more sense. It wasn't my parents reaching out from the beyond in a last attempt to fix our broken family; it had been just the law. I left the law office, got in my car, and drove slowly to the house, where I parked. Getting out and staring up at the yellow paint that looked untouched by the years. I walked slowly up the front stairs, my hand trailing on the handrail that must have been added since I was evicted.

The inside of the house matched the creepy immaculate condition of the exterior. No signs of me could be found throughout the house, not a picture or remnant that the people who lived here ever had a daughter. As I went through the house methodically, checking for unpaid bills or family heirlooms, I tried to stay disconnected. When I reached my old bedroom, I found the door closed and padlocked shut. I looked at the keys dangling from my belt loop, but none bore the symbol of a master lock. My first real emotion broke across my face as I smiled.

"Don't worry, Father, I know how to open locked doors now," I spoke into the silence of the hallway. I stepped back and, with a sense of euphoria, I slammed my boot against the door near the lock. The wood door splintered, but the hinges held. The idea of the looks on my parent's faces if they had there egged me on. I smashed my boot into the door again, this time sending it crashing open. I stepped into the haze of dust. My eyes fell on my old green blanket, the one I had yearned for years ago, strewn across my made bed with a thick layer of dust covering it.

I stepped over to the window, opening it to air out the room. I froze with my hand on the seal. I closed my eyes, greeting the memory instead of fighting it. A young man's face filled my memory, and anger rose at the sight of him. He was rapping at the window, a grin on his face, a small box in his hand as he perched on the roof. I shook my head; it had been Violet's brother Grayson. I stepped back away from the window, looking down at the side table, opening its drawer, and looking for the box. I looked into the bare drawer, then turned to the dresser, its top cleared of my old knick-knacks and pictures. I ignored the stare of my parents' god on the wall above it as I opened the drawers to find them empty. I stepped into the closet, which was also empty. Everything that would have been in the burn pile was missing, so why was the door locked, I wondered. I paused in the middle of the room, then looked back at the bed with a sly smile. I walked to it, pushing the mattress, sneezing as dust danced around my face. I looked down at the box spring, then pulled back the film of fabric to expose the wood beneath and a shoebox jammed between the rungs.

I took the box downstairs and set it on my mother's dining room table, the one I wasn't allowed to touch unless I was setting it for a family holiday dinner. I pulled the lid off the box to find my hodgepodge of items that would have surely got me locked in the basement, or a beating so good I wouldn't go to school for a week. I pulled out a tube of ruby red lipstick, setting it on the table, followed by a copy of Harry Potter. "Devil's work," my mother's voice echoed in my head. I set it aside and pulled out a few pictures of Violet and me and one of Grayson with a heart drawn around his head. I scrunch my nose, wondering why I hadn't destroyed that one after he had told my mother where Violet and I were hiding out, which had resulted in the scrub down to rid me of the sin and punishment to never speak to Violet and her whoreful ways for as long as I lived under my parent's roof. For the first time, I wondered where Violet had gone. Her family had been run out of town similar to the way I had, shamed out for not being the right kind of faithful followers that they should be.

The small box sat in the shoebox next to a pack of gum and a decrepit candy bar. I pulled it out and opened it to find a dried flower and five small white rocks with the letters of the word "sorry" written on them in Sharpie. The box fell from my fingers as a memory slammed into my mind. I was being dragged by my hair now, my mouth unable to call out, something fabric-like lodged between my teeth. The pain in my head made my eyes stream with tears, blurring my vision. I flailed, trying to pull free, my left leg caught in a rose bush. My purple dress was tearing, my skin ripping open, blood seeping from angry scratches as the thorns gleamed at me in the light of the setting sun. My blood made them look menacing as my elbows scratched through white rocks briefly and through a doorway.

I looked down at the rocks strewn across the table and the flower now in pieces. I carefully collected everything from the small box and turned to the front door. I needed to talk to the sheriff, I thought wildly. I exited the house, hesitating for a millisecond when I spotted Minister Jacob Ophesten standing next to my vehicle, peering through the window. He looked old, much less menacing than I remembered. I walked down the stairs confidently, ignoring his smile when he turned.

"Welcome to Samsonton," he greeted with a wide creepy smile.

"Pass," I replied turning my nose up to him.

He frowned.

"If you'll excuse me, Minister, I have an appointment with a rock and roll band who are interested in buying this home," I lied, chuckling as I shut the door to my car behind me and nodded politely at his horrified face as I drove away. He would eventually figure out who I was and call upon the town to push me out. But until then, I needed answers. I reached the sheriff's office at around four o'clock. I clutched the box to me and stepped inside the building. A woman who looked vaguely familiar looked up from a receptionist's desk and smiled politely at me.

"I need a word with the Sheriff," I requested tucking a stray hair behind my ear.

"May I ask what it's regarding?" she asked, typing away at her computer.

"A cold case from 2005," I responded folding my hands together on the counter.

She looked at me curiously, then picked up her phone and talked quietly into the receiver. "Head on back," she informed me, drawing my attention away from a wall of old missing posters. I walked with my head held high, nodding at two deputies who sat at a desk nearby. I twisted the old bronze handle and pushed the door open. I took a step inside, pausing as a growl greeted me. It was low and deep. I looked down, my eyes falling on a large old black lab with gray hair on its crown and muzzle.

"Hunter," I gasped, dropping to my knees in front of the huge dog. I could never forget his big soulful eyes. His tail thudded, and he greeted my hands with a lather of his tongue. I felt my eyes prickle with tears.

A chair squeaked, and I looked up as the sheriff rose to his feet. I felt my jaw drop slightly. This was not the sheriff who had tried to help me. This man was tall with chocolate brown eyes and a tuft of black hair messy on his head with black stubble on his cheeks. He froze, staring at me. Hunter knocked me back as he tried to climb in my lap.

"It's good to see you too, boy," I greeted, scratching him behind his ears. I wiggled free and stood up, my eyes locked with the sheriff.

I swallowed, a blush creeping into my face as I recalled the last time I had seen this man. He had saved me and carried me naked into the hospital. He had even been held for a few days for questioning.

"Abigail…" he breathed.

I smiled, the blush burning on my cheeks. "Thank you," I sputtered nervously.

He smiled. "No need to thank me. Hunter did the hard work, and he has been rewarded," the man informed me, gesturing to a framed letter in my neat handwriting. "Please, have a seat ma'am. My name is Gadreel, Sheriff of Samsonton. Welcome back," he said, staring at me. I took a seat, overwhelmed by the emotions pulsing through me. "How can I help you, Abigail?" he asked after a long staring match.

"I have come to implore you to help me solve my assault," I requested. His eyebrow shot up at my words, and I set the box on the desk. He eyed it, then carefully pulled it to him. "I have not been back until requested to deal with my parent's estate. But since I have been back, repressed memories have been returning to me," I explained, folding my hands in my lap to get them to stop shaking. He looked up from the rocks and rose that littered his desk. "I can walk you through everything I know," I said, watching him. I looked at his face, trying to read his expression. It looked doubtful. "Please, I just want closure," I pleaded.

"Why would you want to put yourself through this again?" he asked, his brown eyes distracting me for a moment.

"I am determined to do this with or without help. I am not weak like I once was. I will not make you save me again," I swore, standing up.

"Whoa, I didn't mean to question your strength. From what I have seen, you're the strongest person I have ever met. Lead the way," he urged, opening the door with a reassuring smile. I led him out and walked side by side toward my house, walking past the back of the churchyard in silence. When we reached the stretch that led to my house, I stopped, glancing up at his face.

"I was leaving choir practice. We had stayed late to figure out how to sing a portion of the song since we lost a singer named Violet when her family was chased out of town," I explained, then stepped forward.

He followed me, watching me. "I was walking home, and the sun was setting. I was humming a song from our selection and had just spotted home when two hands grabbed me and dragged me into this park," I said, turning to the park. I walked through the park, through a once well-worn path that has overgrown in the years past. I pushed through, staring at the side of the house I was staring at. It looked worn down, old, and haunted. I looked to the right and began to walk toward where I knew the hideout was at the far end of the property in the trees. "I was dragged by my hair, gagged with some sort of fabric through here," I explained as we walked through the trees.

We stopped, looking at a shack standing with a broken fence, overgrown with weeds now, but had once been painstakingly painted pink and surrounded by white rocks that Violet's father had brought from California and beautiful rose bushes with various colored flowers adorning them.

"My leg was shredded by a thorn bush as I was pulled in there," I explained, pointing.

He stepped past me, opening the door that fell apart in his strong hands. Within the shack, we found a skeleton long since picked free of flesh, with a pistol nearby, slightly hidden by the overgrowth of foliage. In the corner nearby were the old remains of a purple dress and the old, crumpled remains of a church songbook. Gadreel pulled me to him then. I didn't need to know anymore who the skeleton belonged to; his face blossomed in my mind as he took my most cherished innocence.

I hid my face in Gadreel's coat, his arms cradling me. He had saved me before; he was saving me now from falling to pieces at the dead remains of Grayson along with an old suicide note blaming me for it all, his family's dismissal from the flock. My refusal to court him when I was clearly made to be his.

Gadreel was my fallen angel, he was and will forever be the only person I need to help hold me up and he draws strength from the idea of the women who crawled from the pits of near-death into his yard all those years ago. He has helped me put to rest the past and helped me cultivate a future where he and I thrive to complete each other's needs and goals through communication and teamwork. When I walked down the aisle a year later Hunter was lying by his side, I found faith again, just not in the traditional way that our town would have preferred. I found faith in the love and the goodness of my fallen angel Gadreel.

7 DRAGON SERPENTS

My family shouldn't have died, not because of me, because I refused to submit. If I had submitted, this world could have crumbled to its knees, but now, with them gone... What is left for me in this wretched place? I had kept my secret. I had protected so many lives unknowingly to them all over this planet. I push away the ashes left of my brother's once mountain of stuffed animals, rising shakily to my feet.

They will expect me to submit now, now that I have nothing to lose. They think I need them to become what I am destined to be. But what they don't know is that I am not a mere submissive. I may have my mother's lineage of submission coursing through my veins, but I have my biological father's as well. They thought I was spawned from her marriage to the mortal; I had let them think that all to protect my secret as promised.

The time for secret-keeping was as dead as the skeletons of my family scattered at my feet. I try to slow my breathing, ease my racing heart, and push back the power threatening to burst from my hands. I swipe my ebony hair back away from my face, yanking a hair tie from my wrist to contain it, and in truth, contain myself. I let out a deep breath, struggling to maintain control. I breathe in ash sweeping up my nostrils. Panic fills me. I try to force a sneeze to repel the foreign material inside the ash back out. But it is in vain. I can taste the magic from the flames, the skin particles of my sister, and the fear she felt in her last breath. She had not died instantly.

Power explodes in my chest, and I scream. My scream pierces the night air, booming into a roar that shatters all the windows in the vacated neighborhood. They had all run in fear of magic, the magic of the Messiah and his gang of gib cats. Men who were so hungry for power, all they could do was rape, murder, and plunder until they had their fill. My green eyes glow, my neck stretches, my back exploding as my wings unfurrow for the first time at full capacity. I feel my hands popping as they distort, magic pulsing away, the discomfort as claws tore from my fingertips. Revenge fills me completely. Deep within, I hear a startled voice asking who I am. I know his voice. My mother had made sure, just in case she was wrong, that he had been slain by the Messiah seventeen years ago.

"I am Malinda, daughter of Pachua. I will avenge the death of my family. You and your rule won't stop me," I hiss inside my mind. I slam my wings down, letting my instincts take control. I may be a half-breed, but as a Serpent Dragon, I was powerful, unmarred by magic.

"We are coming," the voice of Pachua hisses into my mind. I can feel his fury, and as he pictures my mother's face, I put on a burst of speed as if to outrun the images ricocheting around my mind. I could feel a sliver of my humanity deep down telling me to slow, to bury my dead, but my sleepy town was far behind me now. If I had let the Messiah and his gang take me, my power would have obliterated the mortals in an instant. But it would be me who would obliterate the Messiah and his gang. As I closed the distance, I could taste the magic in the air and all their defenses as they failed.

I banked around the dark walls of Messiah's castle. I shot straight up into the air, bursting through the ominous cloud above. Dragons scattered as I flipped, ignoring their old worn scales, not admiring their wingspans grown from years of experience. I caught sight of Pachua for a blink, then shot toward the ground at breakneck speed. I felt them behind me, but I was the fastest, maybe because I was young, or because I was powerful. I tucked my wings in and landed on my front claws, the ground shattering beneath my feet, the walls of the castle toppling with a swish of my serpent tail. Messiah froze, his hands raised in defense.

"I am Malinda, you killed my family," I hissed. I see his shield drop as shock consumes him. Then I struck, devouring him and his magic with one bite. "The city is yours," I hissed at my father.

I shot into the air, back to the ashes of my family, dragging my claw across the backyard and using my wing to lay their bones in the cold earth. I covered them with fresh soil, knowing that if I changed back, Messiah would be free. I could never return to my human form.

8 FINDING NORTH

I opened my eyes, pain slicing across my forehead. Groaning then lifted my face off the graveled ground. I pushed myself up into a sitting position, my head pounding, the world swirling around me. I blinked, letting the green trees lining the road stop dancing in my vision. I breathed in, a dull ache greeting me. I watched my breath float into the air, transfixed by how loud it was just floating there and then disappearing. The noise continued growing louder.

My eyelids feel heavy, and my brain feels like roadkill soup. I heard a horrible crunching sound to my right and willed my head to move in the direction of the bone-chilling noise. I was met with chrome shining my blurry face back at me. I grabbed the cold metal, my hands shaking. I pulled myself up one hand after another, a warble of noise ricocheting around my mind. I reached a smooth dark blue metal with a metal emblem that blurred in and out of my vision. The movement distracted me, and my head tilted toward a garbled voice. I opened my mouth, but no words came out. The world tilted, and my eyelids slammed down. I had a sensation of floating, a gentle rocking sensation, then darkness.

A scream ripped from my mouth, followed by pain tearing at my throat. My eyes darted around the yellow room, the walls encrusted with wallpaper from floor to ceiling. I lunged for the side of the bed, vomiting onto a dark hardwood floor. I frowned down at the mess riddled with what looked like miniature rocks.

"Oh dear, here, aim toward this," a woman's voice offered.

I tried to jolt away from the approaching woman only to snag on my IV line and topple out of the bed I had been lying in.

"Ash! Coal!" the woman bellowed.

I held my head as her voice seemed to ping-pong around my skull. I laid back on the hard floor, winded, my body riddled with pain. I blinked, trying to focus my mind, wondering where the trees had gone. I heard a thundering noise, and I pulled myself up, clawing toward the window seat where numerous pillows sat with dogs on them. I stared at the pillows as the sound grew closer. I grabbed my head, remembering the chrome near the trees.

"Eme, what happened?" a voice asked as two men crashed into the room.

I backed toward the pillows. I swallowed hard, fear filling me instantly. My eyes darted around me, looking for something to defend myself with. One of the men caught sight of me first and held up his hands, elbowing the man to his side, who looked over, his jaw-dropping and clutched my hands into fists.

"Mommy, you woke up sissy," a small boy announced, pushing his way between the two men staring at me. My eyes met the little boy, and he smiled. "Good morning, ma'am. Are you feeling better? My chicken laid a nice egg this morning. I am sure my mama could cook it up for you, and you would feel so much better," he offered.

I nodded slowly, opening my mouth to respond. "Please," rasped from my throat. I coughed and then groaned as my body pulsed with pain, the adrenaline leaving my body. I felt hands on me, and I tensed, which made everything hurt worse. Then I was gently set into the bed I had just vacated. My eyes left the retreating boy and locked onto big blue eyes like pools of lake water speckled with stones and gleaming from the light of the sun.

"Are you okay?" the man asked.

"I don't like swimming," I replied thickly in a hissing whisper.

He smiled. "Noted, no swimming in the schedule," he replied, looking over at the woman.

"I will make you something in a moment, dear. My name is Ember Holthearth. These are my brothers, Ashton and Coalton," she informed, gesturing first to the man closest to the door and then to the man next to me. "You are in Bramwell, West Virginia, at Bramwell's care facility," she explained bustling around the room.

I felt myself frown. Care facility? Is that why my whole body felt like I got plowed down by a herd of rhinos? I swallowed hard and tried to avoid the blue eyes to my left.

"What's your name?" Ashton asked, stepping closer. His eyes were also bluish but with streaks of green. I shook my head then opened my mouth to respond but stopped. I felt the frown form on my face again and looked at each of them in turn, then shrugged. I reached for my pockets and found that I was in a hospital gown. I felt the heat in my cheeks as I pulled a blanket around me.

"You don't remember?" Ember asked, glancing at Coalton. "We could have the sheriff run your prints. He is a friend of Coal's, then we can find your family quick as a whip," she offered. I nodded, agreeing silently, staring at my hands. "You rest. I will go make you some food. Coal, go and get Dylan. Ash, could you keep her company?" she directed. Ashton took a seat at the window with the dog pillows, and Coalton rushed from the room, followed by Ember.

"Eme is a great doctor. You'll feel better in no time," Ashton assured sitting back in his chair.

"Thank you," I whispered closing my eyes for a long moment before looking at him again.

He grinned at me and nodded. I laid back on the pillows, trying to remember my name, trying to remember my age, or my favorite color, or even my hair color. I reached up, trying to pull some of my hair into view, but it was too short.

"Excuse me," I whispered to Ashton. His eyes met mine, and I remembered the forest dancing by the road. "What color is my hair?" I asked curiously. His eyes looked sad, but he glanced at my hair and then back at my face.

"Raven black," he informed. I nodded, trying to remember my hair. I must have had it my whole life; why couldn't I remember what color it was? I looked back at Ashton to ask about my eyes, but sleep pulled me into its clutches.

I was woken sometime in the night, unaware of how long I had been asleep. I looked at the pillows in the window seat; Ashton must be long since gone. I heard the sound of crying and voices hollering outside. I sat up, happy that my head felt clearer. The yelling grew louder, and the crying wore on. I got to my feet, the cold floor causing me to hesitate until another cry reached my ears. I moved to the door, aware that my IV line was pulling at my hand. I pulled it free, applying pressure to my hand as I moved. I slipped out of the slightly ajar door and down a pristine hall. I made it to a staircase and descended to the floor below, glancing over the rail to another level below. I continued down another hall; this one had family photos on the walls. I rushed toward the howls and cries. I pushed into a dark room lit by a unicorn lamp's soft glow. I stepped to the crib of the screaming baby, looking down at her scarlet red face.

I felt arms wrap around my leg, and I looked down at the small boy who had been so kind to me. "She is scared," he whimpered. I reached down and picked her up carefully. Shouldn't some sort of instinct kick in on how to soothe a baby? I carried her to the rocking chair, leading the boy with us. "Daddy's back and he sounds like he's been playing with the glass bottles again," the boy whispered, covering his ears as a loud bang and voice came from the floor below.

"What's your name?" I whispered glancing back to the door.

"Orion," the boy responded wiggling nervously as the voices grew louder.

"Do you think you can sing your baby sister a song in the closet while I go get your mommy?" I asked, looking at a walk-in closet across the room. He nodded, and we moved to the closet. I knocked stuffed animals off the shelves and had Orion sit in them, and I handed him his baby sister. "A big happy song," I said.

He began to sing the ABC song, and I closed the closet door. My eyes scanned the room. I moved the rocker in front of the door of the closet and then headed out and to the top of the stairs where the crash of breaking glass echoed up to me. I descended, listening to a man's voice grow louder. I paused in the shadows, leaning and peeking around the corner. Ember was pinned against a wall. A sizeable hairy man brandished a knife and held her by her neck.

"Where are my children?" he bellows spit flying from his furious lips.

Before I register what, I am doing, I have a sturdy vase with red and cream swirls clutched in my hands. I am behind him in what feels like an instant. With all my might, I smash the vase over his head. The knife falls from his hand, and Ember slides to the floor gasping. The man reaches for the knife, screaming in anger. I grab the back of his shirt, yanking the man back towards what I assume is the front door. He flails, blood oozing from his head as I drag him. He finds his feet and gets up. My hand grabs an umbrella from a stand near the door as he lunges at me. I strike him around the face, then smash the side of one of his knees. Red and blue pierce the night through the open door and down the road. I look over at Ember, who is trying to get up. I grab the corner of a large bookshelf and pull it, backing out of the way as it smashes down on the man. I climb over it and step to Ember, putting a handout to help her up.

She looks up at me, tears streaming down her face. I hear a groan. "The children are in the nursery closet," I hissed and walked towards where the man is pulling himself out from under the mess of broken wood and books. He is on his knees, trying to get up when I reach him. I place my foot on his rear and shove him out the door and onto the porch, police cars swinging into a circular driveway. I see trucks just behind them.

"Hands up!" an officer orders. I turn to see who they are talking to, then feel myself being slammed into a pillar on the porch. I scream out, my battered body trembling as adrenaline leaves, and my injuries scream out reminders that I am not fully healed. "Don't move, stop resisting," an officer demanded as metal cuffs pinched my wrists.

"What the hell are you doing here, Patrick?" I heard Coal's voice bellow.

"He tried to hurt Ember," I gasped still struggling to be free, even as the main lances through me.

"What?" the officer holding me demanded, pushing me harder into the pillar. Patrick rolled, groaning. He looked worse in the light of the porch and police lights. I was yanked back and dragged toward the stairs, the gown I wore hanging off one arm, my bruised and battered body gleaming in nothing but a bra and underwear. Coal's furious gaze fell on me, and he stepped forward.

"Let her go," he demanded, trying to cover me with the ripped fabric.

"She was obviously here as an accomplice," the officer refused, then pushed me into the side of the cruiser. I felt the officer's hands release me and glanced over my shoulder to see Coalton's strong arms pulling him back.

"She's Ember's patient. Don't simply jump to conclusions," he demanded. The officer looked over at the Sheriff, who was dealing with Patrick.

"You know you're not a cop anymore, right?" the officer muttered, un-cuffing me.

"I can still kick your ass, Wally," Coalton snarled, shrugging his coat off. I rubbed my wrists, looking up when his jacket was put over my shoulders and pulled around me. It smelled of spices and wood. I had to admit it was quite intoxicating and way too distracting. "Where is Ember?" he asked.

"In the nursery. I had Orion hidden with the baby so I could find Ember. When she was able, she went to them," I explained in my hoarse voice.

He stared at me, then looked back towards the house.

"She might need a doctor," I suggested, remembering her pinned to the wall.

I felt his hand in mine. He pulled me toward the house, gently around Patrick's mess and in the front door. He paused, and I squeezed past, climbing over the bookshelf and holding my hand out to him. He followed. I yelped as I stepped on a piece of the broken vase. His strong arms picked me up and carried me to the stairs, where he set me down, and I followed him up to the second floor. The nursery door was shut. He reached for the door and pushed it open; it caught on something and stopped. He shoved at the door.

"Wait," I requested. I squeezed in the open door, looking at the changing table and dresser blocking the door. I pulled the furniture back, then moved as the changing table toppled over. Coal walked in, and I reached to open the door to the closet, light spilling out around us as I did. There sat Ember, her eyes bloodshot, her lip fat, and marks across her neck causing me to pause.

Coalton knelt, "Hey, Eme."

"She saved me, I mean us," she cried, cradling her two children. I heard feet pounding on the stairs, and I turned toward the door. Ashton barreled into the room, his eyes raking over me before turning to Coalton and Ember.

"We need to get her checked out," Coalton told Ashton.

"Can we come out now, North?" Orion asked. Everyone turned to look at me, who I assumed he was talking to.

"You must have sung the best happy song ever," I replied as he wrestled out of the stuffed animals and hugged my leg.

"I was a good big brother, right, North?" he asked.

"Who is North?" Ashton asked, eyeing me.

"She is. Grandpappy always said that if I ever felt scared or lost that I had to look for the North Star and everything would be okay," Orion explained. I felt all eyes on me, and I shrugged, unaware of how to respond.

Colton rose. "Ash, take Lyra so I can help Eme up," he directed. I watched as Ashton took baby Lyra like a pro. "North, can you hang out with Orion upstairs while we phone the nurse to come help us out?"

"Yes, sir," I agreed and led Orion out of the nursery and quickly up the stairs.

"I'm tired," he whined softly.

"There are some super comfy-looking dog pillows in my room. Want to see if they will help make good dreams?" I asked. He hooted and rushed ahead toward my room. I looked at the walls that are embellished with sweet, painted calming photos, very different from the floors I had seen where the family lived.

My head pulsed, and I paused mid-step. I needed to leave and get back to check-in. I frowned then shook my head as the brief breeze of an idea whisked from my mind. Orion sat in a pile of pillows in the corner of my room. My knees felt weak suddenly, the power leaving my body, and I slumped onto the bed.

"I'll rest over here. Sleep well, North," Orion's small voice said.

It doesn't feel like sleep as the darkness folds in on my mind. It feels like the end. But I can't do anything to stop it, even if my worn body has healed completely. Was this how it would end? It's not so bad, I considered, staring at the ceiling above. Darkness depleted my vision, and a low hum muted my ears.

"Night." I attempted to respond, but if the words left me, I'll never know,

9 FROSTBITTEN BY DESIRE

"Kena! You better be on the damn way! I need my dress!" my sister shrieks, causing me to jerk the sound button on the car to the left flinching.

"I have the dress, all the alterations were made, he just took forever. I will be there even if I have to drive all night."

"Yes! I will go call everyone else and tell them the wedding is on! Best sister ever!" My sister's squeal, less punishing this time, still makes me cringe but I shake my head and smile. Mumbling in the background makes me roll my eyes. This woman couldn't just end a call with me? "Hey Kena, Jameson said be cautious of the weather. His groomsmen are on their way here and they have been listening to the weather. I guess there is a storm pushing in."

"They sound pretty boring if they are just listening to the weather while they wait for news about the biggest event of your life," I tease slowing as the speed limit decreases as I go through a small town. "Hey I need the GPS, I will be there ASAP. Tell Jameson to keep you entertained."

Giggles are the only response I get before the call cuts off and my music kicks back on. My GPS shines from the dash. I slow at a gas station, knowing that with 427 miles to go I would need fuel for me and my Dodge Charger. When I exit the car, there is no hesitation in my stride as I move into the small building, quickly gathering snacks, water, and what I hope is not crappy coffee from a steaming pot.

"Anything else for you dollface?" a tall man asks, giving me a melting grin as he sidles up to the checkout counter, his lean body clad in overalls, grease staining hands that look like they could handle my curves. His attention shifts to a man behind the counter, another Adonis for sure, this one in plaid with green eyes that I could picture idolizing me as I ride him into submission.

My phone rings, pulling me from my wickedly stimulating images of these two sharing me in the backroom. "This is Kena," I answer, stepping up to the counter.

A screech pierces my ear and I yank the phone away pushing the power button, and glaring down at Izzy's name flashing on the screen that reads: CALL ENDED.

"Sounds like your friend is in need of some down time." The mechanic hottie chuckles, his eyes tracing down my body. Lingering on my fitted black jeans.

"She probably needs her brains screwed out and a Xanax."

The cashier drops my chips, his mouth opening in astonishment at my crass words. I feel the fizzle of excitement leave the air. The mechanic may be interested but the cashier wouldn't be easily swayed and it wouldn't be worth my lost time for a subpar orgasim from inexperienced men, no matter how good looking.

"Can I get 30 on pump two please?" I ask, watching the handsome man's cheeks darken red.

The TV behind him begins to make squeaky sounds and my eyes shoot over to the red header on the news channel that reads:

WINTER STORM WARNING

I pull my wallet out, ignoring the mechanic's look of concern as he spots the gun briefly visible by my quick movement.

"That will be $47.58."

With a quick swipe of my card, I accept my groceries, looking at the men again. Though their smiles are gone, their handsome faces both turn to me. "If only…" I sigh, exiting the building and moving to my car to pump my gas, depositing my bag of snacks in the passenger seat after starting the pump. I work to squee-gee my windshield before glancing toward the gray sky.

Pulling the nozzle free from the tank, I put it back in its cradle and close my gas cap securely.

"Hey beautiful," a man greets, walking away from his car and toward me with a wide smile.

"Evening, Frank. Pump your gas and leave the young lady alone," the mechanic orders as he passes us as he moves to his tow truck. I catch him as he glances back at me and then over at the man, his brow creasing in concern.

Popping open the trunk, I grab my work jacket from the trunk and then get into the car. After double checking the GPS, a knock at my window garners a glare from me. The man, Frank, stands there with a large brown paper bag, which looks as if sheaths a fifth of some sort of liquor.

"Care to share?" he yells, wagging the package at me through my window.

I shake my head then plug my phone in, and take a sip of my coffee.

"Come on now, you can have fun hanging out with Franky. I am real nice!" the man bellows at my window, his hand reaching for the handle to my door.

I flick the lights and siren button on my control panel– it's quick but startling. The man backs away, quickly colliding with the pump before rushing over to his car. I watch him for a second as he swigs at his drink and angrily gets in his beat up sedan.

I type in the description, his first name, and his plate before sending it to the local PD. I, then, push my computer back down to resting mode just before starting my car with a roar. It's just my luck that the GPS is going the opposite way as the man who, I hope, will soon be in lock-up. After maneuvering my way out of the small town, I speed up, cranking the music, ready to set a land record to make it to my sister before it gets too late. Hopefully the storm will shoot over.

The first 300 miles are pretty boring with no traffic. As I pushed into the last 127 mile stretch after a very quick restroom break, fluffy snowflakes begin to assault the windshield as I get up to speed after leaving the rest area.

"I should have taken the truck," I growl, slowing slightly, but undeterred.

The snowflakes are fat and fast, the roads quickly turning into white death traps. Eventually, I am at a crawling pace. Even with my windshield wipers oscillating at top speed, they still can't keep all the

snow off my windshield. My GPS tells me that I am only about ten

miles out, but the roads are a mess. The next turn I make leads me up

a slight incline and through twists and turns toward my destination. I

am forced to shift into low gear, turning my fog lights on and sitting

forward looking out into the winter hellscape, placing my trust in the

GPS to show me where the near invisible road is.

About three miles out, I have to pull over. The road is now

impossible to continue driving on. No one has come through with a

plow, and the snow has only gotten worse. I can't see anything in the

darkness beyond my lights, the white out of snow blocking

everything out in all directions.

"Hey Google, call Lily." I growl knocking back the rest of

my water. When I don't hear a response I glance at my phone to see

a "no signal" message pasted on the screen. "Shit."

I smack the steering wheel, pulling my laptop up from its

resting space. It swivels to me then locks in place. With a few clicks

I attempt to rouse my hotspot, but the storm must be shitting on my

signal. I do have a message that must have come through before signal ended that had a retrieval notice of arrest for the man from the gas station, but that does me no good.

The car chimes and I look at the GPS which still shows my route but has a swirl of color that says recalculating route. I frown looking at the dash to find the gas light on. There is no way I can sit here and wait this out. Even if I don't freeze to death, it's almost certain that the snow plow will crush my car if it *does* come up to clear a path. My attention moves back to the storm raging around me, then to the steering wheel. I start to wonder if I can get it to crawl any further, but I quickly change my mind once I remember that it will only waste what little bit of gas I still have.

I twist my phone to take a picture of the map before sticking it into my bra as I look in the back to see what I have in the car to help keep me warm. I know that I have no other choice. I have to make the rest of the trek on foot. Three miles on foot was nothing for me, but three miles in the snow, in my work boots *and* my favorite black jeans wouldn't get me far. I look distastefully at the flattering blouse I am wearing. Reaching back, I drag my duffle to me. Knowing that I won't be bringing it with me, I dig through it for items of clothing that will be my most optimal options for layering up the best I can before getting out of the warm car. I remind myself that I need to hurry before the snow is impossible to travel through on foot as I pull out a sweater that reads *Pioneer Valley Academy*. Setting it aside, I pull on a long sleeve shirt and t-shirt before I jam my arms into the sweater, shrugging my light coat on before wrestling my work jacket on. I pause as I have an idea for one additional layer. I work my way out of my layers just before crawling into the backseat to pop the seat down so that I can grab my kevlar vest. It will weigh me down, but it sure as hell will help hold in the heat at my core.

I redress with the sweater and jacket before managing in the tight space to remove my boots. I wrap my feet in a space blanket from my first aid kit before putting on 3 pairs of socks. I finally jam my oversized feet into my boots and lace them up tight. Rifling in the glove box, I find the riding gloves that I periodically wear when it gets cold back home. They won't be much help for warmth, but I'm hoping carrying my sister's massive dress will be of assistance in that department.

My next step is to activate two hand warmers that I pluck from my first aid kit just before I stow it in my waterproof backpack, along with my toiletries and remaining food and phone charger. By the time I am ready to get out, the snow is up to the door handle, and I wonder for a beat if I had taken too long.

"Get your ass moving, Kenna," I tell myself, flicking on my police lights to warn anyone that might be coming up the road that my vehicle is there.

When I manage to shoulder the door open, the frigid air stings my cheeks. I shove the hand warmers in the back pockets of my pants. I *do* have to protect my best asset, after all. Freeing the seat cover, I wrap it around my head, the warmth from my heated seats soothing my face. Then, I pull out the plastic bag and wedding dress from the car, throwing it over my head to protect me from the onslaught of snow and wind.

Finally, I turn to move towards where the chateaus will be. All I have to do is follow the road. I click on an LED light on my work jacket and march forward. The sounds I make, every ragged breath, and crunch of my boots is muted, first by the howling winds and then by the thunder of my heart beat in my ears.

My lips tremble and sting as the moisture within begins to freeze, ice coats my eye lashes. My hands feel as though they're locked up in frozen death grips on my sister's dress. As I walk further, a soft glow is my only beacon. I push myself on, not sure how far I've gone, I don't know how much longer I can keep going. Suddenly, my guiding light flickers for a moment. Then it blinks out.

"No…" whooshes from me like a death rattle. My feet stumble, the ice making them slide faster. Panic finally snags my heart in Jack Frost's wicked clutches. My body collides with a solid surface, my boots slipping beneath me. I flail out one arm clutching the dress to me and my hand catches on what feels like a handle. Fumbling for a latch, I push down and then shove hard. It doesn't budge. I barely feel my fist as it comes up and I slam on the door, my arms reluctant. I pull out my gun trying to find the lock so I can blast it and gain entry.

The door jerks open and a tall figure appears, but warmth wrenches my body forward. The man backs away, throwing his hands up. I shove my gun in its holster and yank the seat cover from around my face, trying to drag the warm air into my frosty lungs. The man darts past me, closing the door with a resounding thump. The sound of my gasps finally reach my numb ears.

"Kenna!" a voice shrieks before a body collides with me, sending me to the floor in a painful heap.

"Lily? Who is this?" a male voice asks as I try to dislodge my sister from my half-numb, half-burning body.

"My dress!" Lily screams, throwing herself at the discarded bag.

"Everyone okay?" Lily's fiancé Jameson asks, holding up a lantern as he enters what seems to be a lobby with wooden walls and sprawling windows, blanketed in snow. "Holy crap Kenna. How did you make it in this weather?"

I shove myself to my feet as my body struggles to rise, my breaths still harsh as I yank off my snow covered coat and tug at my freezing cold sweatshirt.

"Let's get her warmed up. Then you can ask her all the questions," a voice behind me says.

I look over my shoulder then up into bright blue eyes.

"I am dead." I gulp letting my spinning mind focus on his chiseled body.

"Pretty sure you're still alive," another voice argues, followed by a chorus of chuckles. I turn following a smile of the blue eyed man to find three more men standing near a doorway all watching me intently.

"Heaven." I grin, still trying to free myself from the wet sweater.

"Kenna, no eating the groomsmen," Lily giggles holding up her dress before hugging it to her.

"Why not?" One of them pouts.

"Eating is the furthest thing from my mind. Bet they could warm me from the inside out however. I'd say 'yes' to that over and over again."

The heat of the eyes on me is nearly unbearable. Strong hands grab my arm, slowing my manic moves. "We can figure that out when you're not dripping wet."

"But dripping wet makes all the yeses better for *everyone*," I argue, letting the blue eyed man lead me toward the group of men, their hungry eyes fighting at the sting of what I might worry is frostbite if I wasn't currently listening to my libido.

Part Two

The evil, wet sweater is freed from my shivering body.

"Is that a bullet proof vest?" a voice asks, deep and gravelly.

I try to find the owner of the delicious sound. Instead, I feel hands pull at my vest. "Velcro on my ribs," I grind out, trying to control my shaking arms to help.

"Relax gorgeous, we can handle it," another voice soothes. This one is from a man with a ginger beard and emerald eyes. The sound of velcro nearly makes me moan, until the heat it had trapped in begins to seep from my body. Shirt after shirt is quickly, but gently, pulled away.

"Hold her from behind as I get these boots and pants off. Both of you, tops off. Share your heat," Mister blue eyes demands.

Very warm, bare skin sears against mine. My weak, exhausted arms rise slightly, wanting to explore the strong bodies and run through the hair of a nearby chest. My boots thump to the ground and strong arms lift me in a bear hug as my socks are jerked from my feet, making me squeal as the cold water splashes my dry toes.

"Your feet are dry?" Mister Blue eyes asks, looking up at me between the men.

"Space blanket and socks," I manage. My chattering teeth gave away the strength I was trying to convey with my face.

"Hurry up Nate. Get her pants off and we can get her in bed," the ginger directs while toweling my hair.

Nate drops my gun belt and grasps my pants and peels them away. "I thought that ass was padding. Damn, it's perfect."

"Nathan!" the ginger chastises, kicking Nate's leg before kneeling before me and running the towel over my body quickly. "Get her in the bed under all the blankets."

"Hell yes to that." I agree, unable to put myself in the bed. I'm set gently into it surrounded by deep chuckles.

"Be good, hellcat. We need to get you warm, not take advantage of you," the ginger explains as he adjusts what looks like a wonderful cock, hiding beneath a pair of cargo pants.

"I promise nothing. Oh my god, you're so warm," I moan, shuffling back against a warm bare chest. The body behind me grows ridged arms holding me away.

"Dude, Kent. Warm her ass up." Nathan demands as he climbs into the bed before reaching down for his pants.

"If she keeps wiggling that incredible ass, she is going to get more than just warm," Kent growls, pulling me flush against him, his long hard cock pressing against the back of my left leg.

"Please let me die like this, surrounded by sexy men and enough cocks to satisfy me in the afterlife," I groan as exhaustion battles with the pool of molten heat between my thighs.

The laughter around me rouses me from my heaven just slightly as another body joins the pile. Unconsciousness envelopes me as my body is consumed by warm flesh, strong hands, and– if the delirium is letting me count properly– four raging hard ons.

When I wake, I'm sweaty and warm. I greet hell like an old friend, stretching to ease some of the pressure before freezing. Limbs untangle from me and the rough tickle of a beard scratches my left arm. Tilting my head I look into the serene face of the ginger bearded man. The man beneath me shifts slightly, his hard length sliding up the back of my leg. I slide my leg a little feeling his girth shift saluting my vagina. A gasp leaves my mouth as my eyes lock onto movement when I see a naked man walk into the room and feed a fire that's crackling happily about 10 feet from the bed.

He turns, brown eyes looking for the disturbance of the near silence. My nipples harden as desire fills his face, his eyes tracing agonizingly slow up my body. Surprise takes over as he reaches my face.

"Um…" He coughs, his gravelly voices warming my core.

"Please, don't change your thought pattern," I beg in a hoarse whisper that makes him chuckle.

"Hellcat, you don't know what you're saying. Go back to sleep."

"So you're all sexy eyes, and no follow through? That blows," I sigh, trying not to move my hips, while the friction of the large cock teases me just outside my molten folds. "If the rest of you are going to deny me, you better move before I screw you all silly."

The words no sooner leave my mouth then laughter surrounds me and I close my eyes in defeat.

"Wouldn't you rather get to know each of us individually? Then choose who you think could satisfy you completely?" the brown-eyed man asks, his voice much closer now.

I open my eyes looking as he crawls over me, the tip of his cock dragging up my leg as he nears my apex.

"One is never my go-to. Sharing *is* caring afterall." The cock between my thighs shifts and a moan creeps from my lips.

"You sure you're feeling okay? Don't need this to be an agreement based on you being dead and all," Tte brown-eyed man teases, his cock pausing at my apex.

He doesn't flinch away from the other dick already resting there and my heart hammers.

"You guys better make sure I have feeling everywhere. That's probably the best bet to make sure I am working properly."

"Mario, if you aren't going to accept her offer, then let me," the ginger says, shifting next to me, his dick slapping my leg.

"What are your no goes, Hellcat?" Mario asks, the head of his cock making small circles near my pulsing heat.

"It's Kenna, and I have none. Tie me up and pick a hole, if you're crafty I am sure you can all fit," I gasp, tilting my head back and arching my back. My body is begging to be touched.

"Well Merry Fucking Christmas to us. Get the hellcat something for her hands, Nate." Mario orders, pressing in ever so slightly before he leans down toward me.

"All our ties are in my room," Nate announces as drawers open and clothes.

I moan. It's a whining sound as my slick beads out of me sliding down onto the body beneath mine.

"She is dripping wet. Just grab something!" Kent groans from behind me.

A hand slides down my stomach as lips caress mine, my hips move to meet the hand as it reaches my wet folds. Long, thick fingers stroke my entrance briefly before two fingers plunge in. The moan that rips from my mouth is swallowed by the mouth above mine.

"Shit, she's so tight. She wants her hands tied. Find anything!" the mouth claiming my own says, his brown eyes boring into mine as he swirls within me.

"Hands up, Hellcat," Nate instructs. I move them as they are unpinned and a rough texture scratches at my skin. I gasp for air, my hips swaying as I break eye contact to look up at Nate and the man beneath me as they secure my hands with fluffy silver and red tinsel. It winds around and around, crisscrossing until my hands look like a fluffy bushel of tinsel.

"She's secure. The safe word is Santa. You got that Hellcat?" he asks, pulling his fingers free.

"Hell yes. Best Christmas ever is what I expect," I respond breathily, I am rewarded with the flash of a smile before his lips capture mine and his length plunges into me. My shriek of pure delight is lost in his dominating mouth.

"Come Hellcat."

"I'm not that easily swayed," I pant back then frown as he backs away slightly without pulling out. The man beneath me pushes up, my legs spreading and my moan swallowed as Mario sinks deeply into me. My bound hands are above us as two large hands grab my breasts.

"What's the safeword Hellcat?" Mario ask rolling his hips as he moves now beneath me.

"No fucking way I am saying that!" I gasp as another cock presses at my heat, punishingly pushing its way into me. The pain is intense. They pause as I gasp, letting me stretch and adjust. I move my hips experimentally, air rushing from my mouth as pleasure curls up my core. The fullness is indescribable.

"That's it Hellcat. Ride them, but lean forward." the ginger instructs, pulling at my nipples as I follow his directions. "What do you need, Hellcat?"

"Nate, join us." I beg, feeling a hand down beneath me for a moment, before it drags up to my anus circling as I puker up. A snarl escapes me. "That now, please." I manage, shivering with anticipation as an all time dream of mine is about to be fulfilled. Nate moves closer his lips capturing my scream as the ginger pushes into me, halting all movement as I adjust once again. My hips buck as my orgasm escapes me and my entire bottom half is puppeteered by the three men filling me to the max.

My toes curl, my wrists sing, and the kiss deepens. I pull back panting as Nate closes the distance, his dick in one hand, my face in his other.

"Put it in my mouth. Now!" I demand, feeling the electricity tingling in my fingers and toes, before the pulsing of my core begins to sing out to my nerves. Nathan moves and I turn my head to accommodate the angle. His large dick approaches and, as he hesitates, I open my mouth and with the momentum of the cock burrowing into my ass I take him hard and fast. I struggle against the tinsel wanting to touch them. Another orgasm flares within me. It's so powerful that it could be triggered by any one of the dicks in me.

The tinsel snaps and my arm shoots out, wrapping around Nate's leg and taking him deeper. The other one reaches for the tangle of bodies around me, dragging across abs and the tangle of chest hairs. Through sweat and heaving muscles. Groans begin to signal the release of heat that begins deep in my core. Almost simultaneously, it is followed by a stream of heat deep in my ass. The streams are then topped off with hot cum coating the back of my throat as I ride out orgasm after orgasm. My body is unable to stop as I light up like a damn firework.

The dick in my mouth slides free, and Nate's lips capture mine before Mario's lips steal me away, his hands clutching my face as he gasps for air. When he pulls free, he yanks the sheet to start cleaning us up. Suddenly, a man I had yet to officially meet but know as Kent, pulls out of me once the ginger is uncorked. He pulls me into his arms and captures my mouth. Tilting my head back, he trails his kisses down my neck as the ginger's lips consume mine.

"How long do we get to keep this christmas gift?" someone asks. Laughter fills the room.

"I dunno about you all, but I am ready to order tinsel in bulk."

"I second that," Mario agrees, getting to his feet.

"I third that," Kent chimes in, accepting a towel from Nate.

"I agree to that as well," Nate sighs, watching me wince but smile.

"100% no returns." The ginger grins.

"I need your name. Calling you my 'ginger sex god' isn't really the best idea when you're recharging."

Heat creeps up his neck but he blasts me with an amazing smile, his beard twitching slightly before one of his hands scrubs at it thoughtfully. "I don't know Hellcat, I really like Ginger Sex God."

Nate laughs, "Just wait till you have had time to get to know us better. You might change one of us to your sex god."

"My blue-eyed Adonis has game. Noted."

Nate grins, glancing at Mario who hands out bottles of water.

"His name is Rudolfo, but he hates it because of Rudolph the Red Nosed Reindeer." Mario explains, running his knuckles down my cheek affectionately before handing me the bottle.

"Thank you, Alpha," I accept cheekily.

"Yes!" Kent hoots, watching Mario's jaw slack slightly.

"Lastly, Clark Kent here. Waking me up with full mast exploration is always appreciated." The laughter flowing around the room makes me smile. The fact that these men are still naked distracts me from their cool down. In the full light of the lanterns and low fire, I finally get to take in their bodies. They are all taller than me, which is not always something guys can do at my 5'8 build.

The sound of my phone ringing distracts me from ogling them. I kick my legs off the bed and the men move in a flurry looking for my phone. "It was in my bra." I offer pulling my legs up and watching as they scour the room for it. Well toned asses, calves, and cocks swinging around.

"Yeah, that means it's on the floor. That thing ricochet off the walls. I *may* have been a little too eager to warm up your ample breasts," Nate explains as he moves around the bed.

"Ample? Man, she called you an Adonis, and *that's* the best you got?" Mario teases, snagging my phone up from the floor and handing it to me.

"Thanks, Alpha." I enjoy the twitch of his cock as he stares at me. "Officer Mckenna Claus," I say as I answer my phone.

"Officer?" Kent whispers looking at the others curiously.

"Claus?" Rodolfo asks just as quietly glancing at the door.

"Is this about the arrest made yesterday after my recommendation?" I ask, annoyance filling my tone at the interruption as my four sex doms stare at me in wonder. "No bail, let him sweat. He was driving under the influence, and *clearly* has boundary issues. He's lucky all I did was startle him with my sirens. I should have kicked his drunk ass for propositioning me and yelling at me. Have a Merry Christmas." I hang up on the officer and look around at the now brooding faces around me.

"Someone messed with you?" Mario asks, his muscles rippling.

"You're a cop?" Rudolpho asks, looking down at my gun belt then back at me.

"You can kick some man's ass?" Kent asks, his curiosity breaking through his grumpy face.

"You're a Claus?" Nate asks, looking toward the door.

I sit back leaning on one of my arms. My eyes dart around the room, taking in the tension, my nipples harden and I capture my lip in my mouth. "If you guys don't calm down, I am going to have to take care of myself before you guys can recharge."

"That's our Hellcat," Mario grins, his hand moving down to his hardening cock.

A knock at the door has bare asses staring at me as my sister's voice pierces the wooden door. "Kenna? How are you feeling?"

"Fanfuckingtastic!" I shout back accepting my dry underwear from Nate. A shirt is pressed into my hand and I slip my arms into the button up moving to the door.

"Can I come in?" Lily yells as I approach the door.

"No." I deny opening the door and leaning on the jam keeping the door snug against my hip, shivering slightly at the cold air in the corridor.

"Did I wake you? Merry Christmas!" She hops foot to foot rubbing her arms and smiling widely.

"Happy Wedding Day," I correct watching as she glows with happiness.

"Do you think you can help me finish decorating so we can get this wedding started? You will be the only bridesmaid but I figured you like it better that way. Santa brought you a woman free miracle!" Lily laughs glancing back over her shoulder.

"Whoa slow down Lily. No reason to be using such a horrible S word on the happiest day of your life." I look back at the men who are silently dressing and wink at them, before turning back to Lily.

"Do you have a guest? You really waste no time. I thought you were too picky for Jameson's friends," Lily laughs as she tries to peek into the room.

"I have needs, Lily. Not all men can handle the pressure."

"Put some clothes on, Hellcat. We can help you and your sister reach up high," Mario teases his hand sliding possessively across my stomach, causing my sister's eyes to widen. I open the door to my clothed men who file out, smiling at Lily, as they each hand me an article of clothing.

"How cold is it out there?" I ask my flustered sister.

"All of them?" She whispers to me, her eyes as round as silver dollar coins.

I slide my black jeans on. They're warm and tight from drying wet next to the fire. "All at once."

"All? How?" She gasps, her cheeks darken and her hands fly up to her mouth.

"Lily! They found the rest of the decorations!" Jameson calls down the hall.

I pull my academy sweater on and snag some socks, tugging them on before checking my boots. They're still damp so I leave them behind before turning to follow my flabbergasted sister.

Part Three

By the time I get down the hall with Lilly, the smell of sausage wafts through the door at the end of the cold hall. We push through a door into a large room with a massive fireplace in the center, surrounded by seats that go in a perfect circle around it. My sex mistros stand around Jameson with enthused voices and wide smiles.

"Yo cannibal, the food you can eat is over here," Lily announces, yanking my attention from the men as I profile who they must be outside of the bedroom.

Four pairs of eyes seek me out, but I only grin and move to my sister's side. We both accept a plate from an older man who kneels beside the roaring log fire with cast iron pans and large oven mitts. "Thank you so much for breakfast, I am famished."

The man smiles. "I should make breakfast like this more often. I can't imagine how everyone is so happy with no power available. I really appreciate everyone being so understanding as we work to get things back up and running."

"Mr. Campbell, we are just so happy everyone is safe. We have dreamed of being married up here since we met two years ago," Lily sighs, reaching out for Jameson.

"I just wish there was heat in the chapel and that your decorations had made it from the storage shed," Mr. Campbell sighs, flipping a pancake onto my nearly empty plate.

I nod, appreciatively chewing the sausage in my mouth, very aware of the frowns of my guys as they all approach and take a seat next to me. Mario holds out a steaming mug to me and I swallow my bite, glancing at his handsome face and then at the cup.

"Coffee?" he offers, his chocolate eyes intense and observant.

"Yes please," I moan, accepting the cup and setting my plate in my lap so I can wrap my fingers around the hot cup and soak in the warmth.

"Need sugar or something?" Nate asks, watching our exchange with interest.

"No thanks. Black is perfect."

"Like her soul," Lilly teases, leaning into Jameson's embrace.

"That sucker is freaking iridescent at this point. I got to normalize it somehow."

"The frostbite that bad?" Jameson asks, an eyebrow shooting up in concern.

"Jameson, she had to have been out there for a really long time," Lilly interjects, looking me over.

"Never said it was from the cold." I grin watching my sister's eyes flick to the four men, now all seated to my right.

"I checked her over thoroughly. She is in pristine condition," Rodolfo says, his eyes locking on mine as my attention shifts to him.

Mr. Campbell flips more pancakes onto plates then waltzes from the room.

"I thought you said you got the decorations? Do we need to go back out into the snow to rescue it?" I frown, not at all wanting to risk the cold again.

"They had their Christmas decor that they'd already taken down. We are going to put all of that back up," Lilly explains, pointing over to a corner filled with overflowing decor.

"No one else was able to make it, so it will just be the 7 of us. Sorry guys. I know I promised that I would introduce you to some amazing women. Lily literally spent *weeks* hand picking her friends for you." Jameson apologizes, then kisses Lilly's forehead.

A giggle slips from my mouth and Lilly rolls her eyes. "Always with the matchmaking, Lily Claus. Leave these men alone."

"Don't worry about it, Jameson. Curious, though, who Lily thought would be best suited with Mckenna here." Mario asks, looking over at the other guys then winking at me.

I look over to my sister and Jameson.

"That wasn't really an option," Jameson denies.

"Why?" I ask tilting my head and looking only at Lilly, who flushes.

"Come on Kenna. You work all the time. These guys hardly make time outside of work as it is. Not a single one of you has a schedule that would compliment the other's. The only time you all have in common is when you lot do guys' night and Kenna dedicates to writing her… adult books." Jameson stumbles over this last part, his cheeks flaring.

"You better spice up this man's life if my smutty books embarrass him," I warn Lilly, polishing off my coffee, and returning to my pancakes.

"You write sex novels?" Kent asks, his tongue slipping across his bottom lip as he waits for my response.

"I *dominate* sex novels," Their eyes darken, making my blood simmer as I sit there, wishing I had them all back in our room now that I was refueled.

"TMI, Kenna!" Jameson chokes, spluttering coffee all over his shirt.

"No such thing. I was asked a question and answered it. Kent deserves an honest answer."

"Ever heard of being too honest?" Jameson asks, wiping at his clothes and giving Lily a look as she laughs next to him.

"You'll have to check out my work sometime. For now, Superman, I think we need to get the decorating started so these two can get hitched. You know, before Jameson knows Lily reads all my books and ends up chickening out." I goad, winking at Kent as I rise to my feet and stretch, a small moan escaping my lips.

"To answer your question I was going to introduce Izzy to Mario. He's not only Jameson's best man, but also the dark haired friend that is watching you so intently," Lilly informs, smirking at Mario.

I glance over. "Izzy called me yesterday. So unless Mario is into really annoying women, that wouldn't have worked out. Alpha, are you into annoying women?" I ask, addressing him as he rises to stand next to me. His fingers burn up my spine as he drags them up.

"No. Usually I'm into submissive bombshells, but I *do* think I have a taste for assertive omegas." The smell of him so close causes my core to clench. I want his lips on me again.

"You talked to Izzy? Was she on her way?" Lilly asks, touching my arm lightly breaking me from Mario's trance.

"She screamed really loud when I answered my phone and I hung up on her. I was going to call her back after she had a moment to calm down, but I had to request an arrest and got distracted. I never got back to her," I admit, watching Lilly frown.

"See? She's a workaholic!" Jameson teases, looking at Mario's proximity to me and quirking an eyebrow at him.

"Ms. Claus, I found the suit. Will this work for what you are picturing for your Christmas wedding?" Mr. Campbell asks Lilly as he walks back into the room. He holds up a lovingly made, red Santa suit. Just the thought of the word Santa makes me inwardly flinch.

"I bet if we get the decorating done, we can fit some down time into the schedule before tonight's wedding." My offer is met by movement as all four men rush toward the boxes in the corner.

"I've never seen *any* of them so quick to help. Thanks guys. Continuously moving will also help all of us stay warm," Jameson announces.

The attention of my guys turns back to me as I step away from the warmth of the fire. Rudolfo takes my hand and pulls me to the side gently, leaning down slightly to look into my eyes. He glances back to the fire. "Shouldn't you stay by the fire and keep your circulation primed after how cold you got yesterday? Getting sick would be no fun for you," he presses further. He releases my hand and grasps my side, a large thumb slipping under my top and across the warm skin on my side.

"I'm not a sideline lady. Guess we will have to figure out creative ways to keep me throughout the day," I challenge, smiling up at him before I look toward the directions of the other three.

"Should we use tinsel?" Lilly asks from an open box, her hands covered in the bright sparking snaking tendrils.

"Yes!" my guys say in unison.

"Sounds like tinsel is a great idea! Where is the wedding going to be?" I ask, looking around the large cozy room.

The warm fingers leave my side after a brief squeeze, and Rudolfo moves over to the guys talking in a low whisper. I know he repeated my challenge by the way they all turned to look at me simultaneously.

"Through this door is the chapel, but without power it's really cold in there," Lily explains, gesturing to the door.

"Shouldn't the door be open so the heat can start warming up both rooms?" I ask as I look over to Mr. Campbell.

"That *would* help. I also want to be sure that everyone can remain safe and comfortable." he agrees, looking around the room.

"So if it becomes unbearable, we would have to shut the doors and postpone?" I ask, looking at Mr. Campbell nod in agreement.

"Why don't we decorate in here?" I interject. Seeing the look on my sister's face, I continue. "Hear me out, Lily. Each of the halls are cold right? Like even when you were just waiting for me to open the door, the air made you *really* cold. So why don't we centralize the ceremony? I mean, it's not like we need all that space now, and the glow from the fire is going to make the pictures look *amazing*."

Lily looks over to Jameson, and then over to Nathan. "Is she right Nate?"

My Adonis' mouth curves up. "She is absolutely correct. The light from the fire will look way better than the LED lights of flashlights in the pictures. It'll make them look amazing, intimate in a way the flashlights wouldn't be able to do."

"Also, this is where you met him. Here at this very fireplace, if I am not mistaken?" I press then look over warily at the chapel door.

Lily nods slowly at first, then walks across the room to the far wall with the tinsel. "I told her the same thing already. Why does she listen to you so quickly?" Jameson asks quietly.

"I am *very* persuasive. Mr. Campbell, do you have a ladder we can access?" I ask, looking over at the relieved looking man.

He nods. "In the chapel– far wall to the right," he informs me as he moves to the boxes to help the decorating commence.

I move to the door, pushing through it with instant regret. The room beyond is deathly cold. "Shit," I hiss as I move through the dark room cautiously. Four beams of light illuminate my surroundings, and I grin without looking back. My fingers connect with the freezing metal of the ladder and my warm fingers burn in response.

"We got it. Rodolfo, it looks like she's cold." Mario smirks as he takes the ladder and lifts it, Kent taking the opposite side. The tag-team as they carry it back toward the door.

"Are you cold, Princess?" he asks from directly behind me.

I spin, prepare to argue that I am not a princess, but I'm immediately silenced as his lips capture mine, his large warm hands snaking around me. Instead of arguing, I melt into him, my cold hands tracing up his shirt tangling into his burly hairy chest.

"She's so cold that she'll need a little more help than that," Nathan's voice whispers in my ear before he burrows into my hair, nipping at my neck and pressing against me. "How can we warm you up? Or are you using your safe word and avoiding being found?"

I gasp away from Rodolfo's expert mouth. "My Sex God *and* Adonis working together to make me warm? I can accept that eagerly."

Nathan moves behind me, one hand unfastening the button from my pants, as Rudolfo pulls me back to him, consuming my mouth as his strong hand tangles itself into my hair.

"Quickly," Nathan urges, pulling me back. The heat of his body then leaves my back side and his hands yank on my pants. I glance at the door, hurriedly trying to force my boot off of my foot.

"No time Omega. You'll have to deal with bound ankles *and* wrists this time," Ruddolfo insists as he pushes me back a step. I look down as he releases me and drops to the floor. Teeth bite at the back of my bare leg, a warm tongue soothing the slight ache. A cock at full attention greeting me, Rudolfo moves my feet one at a time before adding his legs to the pair below me. He, then, scoots cock to cock with Nathan, taking my hand and tugging me down immediately after.

"Sink down, Princess. Let us get you all warmed up," Nathan urges, his hands now on my hips.

I sink onto Rudolfo's thick cock, wondering how he had managed to get this amazing appendage in my ass, before pulling myself up by grasping their shoulders and sinking onto Nathan's head spinning length. I twist my body, panting as he captures my lips. My fingers grasp Rudolpho and I pull myself back up off of Nathan.

"Keep her mouth busy so no one can hear her," Nathan instructs, reaching down to grasp their cocks and line them up.

I grin, eagerly welcoming my sex god's lips as his hands reach around to cradle my ass. He holds me there for a moment, kissing me breathless, until the drips of my folds slip from me. He lowers me and I spread my legs to help ease the discomfort as pleasure burns through me, all thoughts of the now pitch black freezing room leave my mind.

Nathan's hands wrap around me, sliding across my stomach as he attempts to allow me time to adjust, but I don't want to adjust. My hands grasp his, forcing them up to my breasts, my moan of needs swallowed in the bearded mouth against mine. Warm arms encircle me. Every move I make shoots pleasure throughout my body. My strong legs angle and my hips sway, a groan behind me urging me on as their grasps tighten, pulling me back down as I ride them. Warmth spreads through my body, sweat beading across my breasts.

"Kenna?" Lilly calls into the dark room, causing me to clamp down. My head rests on Rudolphos shoulder as I pant, my hips do not stop moving the fiction dragging across the my tight walls making me want to scream.

Mario's deep voice urges her from the door and it closes basking us in darkness, a renewed urgency filling me once again. These addicting men are going to need to be ridden properly later. I needed to be helping my sister, even if they end up chickening out on going through with this for a third time.

"Who has the tinsel?" I gasp, my nails digging into Rudolpho's shirt.

"Hands up Omega," Nathan whispers and I follow his directions, letting my sex god's strong hands lift and drop me on their swollen cocks. The scratch of the tinsel and then pinch of my wrists garners a growl as my body pleads for the intense orgasm that is building inside me.

"That's it, Baby. Let us fuck you to your climax," Rudolfo urges, his beard tickling my face before they both buck up into me.

I nearly scream out but I clamp my teeth shut. A hot mouth and tantalizing tongue pulls at my shoulder blade as Nathan's hands latch back onto my tits like a vice, squeezing and teasing as they assault my core with a rhythmic dance of pulsing cocks, feeling as if they grow larger with every synchronized move. My entire body trembles and I shatter, my mouth once again captured by my sex god as my body explodes with ecstasy. He groans into my mouth as Nathan grunts behind me and hot seed sends me into an immediate orgasm as my hips move and I try to drag them both in deeper. I suck them dry with my eager pussy until the three of us are a panting heap and the chill begins to tickle at the sweat covering my body.

"We better head back. It's been almost 20 minutes, beautiful." Rudolph sighs as he places one last kiss on my lips.

"Leave me here to melt," I groan back, the sound of their laughter tugging at my lips.

"Well Doll, you have us latched down deep and secure." Nathan laughs his hands releasing my breasts and tracing down my body teasing my clit causing my muscles to clamp them within me tighter. "I need to remember that button. Damn Kenna. How are you even able to constrict your glorious heat? Especially after it has been put through such a beating today."

I lean back to kiss his cheek and then push myself to my feet, unlocking them. A flashlight beaming by my feet lets me take in the glorious tangle of limbs that belong to two of my new obsessions. "Not sure you four are prepared for what you've gotten yourselves into. Maybe it's *you* lot that should have a safe word. Better have a chat with Alpha and Clark Kent. You all might get tired of trying to subdue my raging libido."

They both stare at me as they untangle and pull their pants on, looking at me as I stand half naked, waiting patiently. "Cover up that amazing body, or I'll have to get the guys in here and you'll be unable to help your sister at all."

I smile, holding out my bound wrists. Nathan breaks the binding as Rudolpho yanks my pants up, his cold nose nuzzling the mouth of my sex before he stands to full height, grinning.

"Let's go get these two ready to get married. If they bail again, you better be ready for my attitude."

They exchange looks and follow me through the dark room, lighting my path. When we enter the main room, we find a mess of tinsel and reindeer statues strewn about as my sister lectures Jameson about everything being perfect. I ignore their discussion, instead taking in the heated gazes of Kent and Mario, who look over from atop the ladder. Time to get this place ready!

Part Four

After getting all of the decorations up and the remains of tinsel fragments swept from the floor Mr. Clark appears with a sullen expression. "It's snowing again, Ms. Claus. If you were holding any hope that the rest of your guests would arrive. you should know that. Not even the plows are running."

"How do you know?" I ask looking around wondering if I had missed the electricity coming back on.

"Ham radio in my room. The plow spotted a police vehicle stuck in the snow and, because of the snow, have decided to fall back. They didn't find the officer. That was about three miles from here," he explains, running a hand through his hair.

"That's my Charger. He didn't hit it with the plow, did he? *That* would be a lot of paperwork," I sigh, plopping down on the couch.

"You walked three miles in the storm?" Mario asks, frowning

I shrug. "I run at least five every morning. The distance wasn't a deterrent. That's why this is happening this time." My attention moves pointedly to Lilly, who looks even more nervous.

"Oh, it's happening. Why don't I grab you some of my clothes? Then, you can go get some rest and afterwards, you can meet me to freshen up and get ready at about 6:00?" Lilly asks, glancing at her watch.

"I boiled some water for washing. We have a back stock. Figured it's time to start preparing for lunch. I am sorry again, Kenna, that I don't have your room available. The roof of that yurt collapsed last night."

"Glad I was safe with you guys, then," I shrug, looking fondly over at the four men to my left and right. They look at one another then over at Mr. Campbell.

"I will help you cook and we can chat about that," Rudolfo offers as he stands up to assist Mr. Campbell, closely followed by Nathan.

Lilly gets up and rushes down a hall to her and Jameson's room.

"We are going to go through with it this time, Kenna," Jameson insists, wringing his hands.

"I hope so. You guys compliment each other's crazy. It's never gonna be the perfect day if you wait for others to fill that void. You control today's outcome, and your future," I lecture, then glance down at my hand where Mario is leisurely running his finger down my palm and wrist.

"Thanks for always supporting our choice Kenna. This is for real *it*. We had hoped you all would be happily fraternizing with some great people and just feeling the love of our special day. I want all my buddies, and you, to all be happy."

"Jameson, it's not about us. Today is about you and Lilly. Let *us* worry about our own wants and needs. Focus on her. Go read one of my books to her," I tease with a glance at my other hand where Kent is hooking one of his fingers with mine.

"Here you go Kenna," Lilly announces as she plops an outfit in my lap, the shoes tucked within, almost toppling to the floor. Her eyes move from Mario's touch to Kent's then back to me.

"Thanks." I grin then look over at Nathan who walks into the room with a large pot, followed by Mr. Campbell. They pass, splitting off and walking back to our room, as well as my sister's room.

"That's our cue to get cleaned up!" Mario insists as his hand claps on my knee, sending a pulse of desire though me.

"Our?" Jameson asks, looking at his friends as they get to their feet.

"I mean, you're the groom. Shouldn't you want to be ready, too?" Mario asks, glancing down at me.

They move toward our room and I grasp the clothes that Lilly brought me. I smirk as she watches me curiously.

"Play nice, Kenna. They are really good guys." Jameson warns, taking Lilly's hand and turning with her to head to their room. I frown after them then glance at Nathan, who exits the hall to our room.

"You okay?" he asks his gaze looking in the direction that Lily and Jameson had just walked toward.

"Your friend is worried that I might not play nice."

"How dare he try to intervene? Just be *you* Kenna. I know we all find you infatuating." His hand runs across my backside and he moves away to join Mr. Campbell as they move into another part of the hotel.

I hug the clothes and move toward our room. We would all need to talk about what their public expectation is. I had no problem people seeing me being shown off by four sexy as hell men. But this thing could possibly be over when we are not so isolated and back to our normal lives. Every ounce of my being sure as hell hopes not. A shiver races through me and I sigh, pulling up short when I nearly collide with Mario.

"You alright, gorgeous?" he asks as he rubs his thumb over my cheek.

"Just a chill from the hall," I assure, letting my rampant thoughts focus on the here and now.

"So you're cold?" Kent asks, placing a log on the fire and turning to me, his gaze heated.

"We can't have that," Mario sighs, pulling his shirt off, his abs rippling from the movement.

"Yeah, I am absolutely freezing."

Kent pulls his shirt off and I can not figure out where to look. It's all muscles and sexyness.

"Strip, Omega," Mario demands, dipping a hand towel into the steaming pot of water near the fire and using it to rub across his torso.

"Yes, Alpha." I grin back as I teasingly take off each piece of my clothes slowly, enjoying their attentive eyes and hardening cocks. When I am completely naked, I stand up proud and waiting for my next directive. They circle me like I'm their prey.

Mario pauses, tucking his finger under my chin, before kissing me. It's a deep heated kiss that ends too quickly. He spins me around and pulls me flush against his hard body, hands sliding down me to cupp my sex before two fingers hook in, swirling around for a moment before sliding back out. My attention moves to Kent who sits on the edge of the bed, his dick saluting me.

"I heard that you have quite the amazing mouth," he greets, his hand stroking up his cock, precum oozing deliciously from its head.

"Amazing *might* be an understatement," I reply cheekily, feeling Mario's fingers wet with my slick slide across my ass hole. They really must be worried they will wear me out, I consider for half a second before a warm hand on my shoulder pushes me to bend over. I follow the lead, arching my back when the feel of Mario's cock slides across my cheeks. My hands slap down on Kent's thighs and I give him a grin, watching his eyes as they track my breasts.

"Sure hope you pull my hair or entertain my breasts while I enjoy my snack."

I watch a moment of surprise flash in his eyes and bend further down, taking him in my mouth, groaning when a stinging slap on my ass cheek rings through the room. Mario adjusts, a clear warning that I might want to halt my tasting exploration. But as Kent's dick hits the back of my throat, I'm too consumed in my mission. Kent makes the most panty wetting groan as his hand fists my hair.

"This wasn't the plan," Mario growls.

I feel his hand slipping between my legs and into my greedy pussy, just long enough to lube up his hand, then he grunts as he begins to push into my ass. I gasp and let the pain out my mouth, rolling my tongue around the lolicock in my mouth. Hands grasp my hips and I steady my stance, pushing back against him so he will take me harder. With his next thrust, Kent moans as he slides down my throat. I suck hard, letting my moans work to my advantage as Mario loses control of his measured thrusts.

Hands latch onto my tits and cum shoots down my throat. "Crap!" Kent grinds out.

I twist my ankle around Mario's and tug him with me, swallowing the full load in my mouth before pushing Kent backward. I shift Mario– and by extension myself– so I can sink down onto Kent, his dick miraculously showing up as I needily begin to rock my hips, my nails digging into his chest.

Kent's jaw drops as my breasts smack into his chest and my hands pull him to me as the moans pouring from my mouth turn to screams of pleasure. He captures my lips with his, finally bucking beneath me.

"Can you reach the tinsel?" Mario asks Kent, who growls as he pulls from my possessive kiss to reach for the tinsel across the bed. His dick drags over my g-spot and I cry out. "Freeze, Kent," Mario demands. "Hands up, Omega."

I release Kent and raise my arms, a cock burrowed into my ass as, deep in my core, Kent's dick continues to assault *just* the right spot. A Large hand locks my wrists together and a knee slides up next to me. Finally, Mario begins to move again, spearing me on Kent's cock and making me scream in earnest.

"Come for me," Mario hisses in my ear, causing me to explode. The orgasm feels endless. As soon as it is about to taper off, another thrust sends me careening into another. Mario grunts and Kent hisses as they fill me with their hot seed. Eventually, I melt onto Kent's chest as I try to drag air into my lungs. Kisses are pressed to my sweaty forehead, and soon enough, I am rolled over and spooned.

Voices rouse me from my nap. I feel the sensation of fingers as they caress my spine, and the chest below me vibrates as its owner speaks.

"How could this even work outside of here? Isn't that just too much skepticism for her?" Mario asks.

My eyelids stay closed as the hushed, arguing voices rise around the room.

"She obviously has no problems with this. What are you worried about?" Nathan asks from behind me on the bed.

"She is a cop. Don't you think she has a reputation that she wants to protect? I would have to kill someone if they called her the names that they undoubtedly would if we keep her."

The word if burns my mind. I would do just about anything to have these sexy men continue to bed me. Even if it's until I die in the heat of sex at a ripe old age, ideally impaled by all of them during my final breath.

"It should really be her choice," Rudolfo argues from nearby.

"I don't know…" Kent sighs.

Stretching, I let a small yawn escape as I wiggle slightly before pushing myself into a seated position. "Did you enjoy your nap?" Mario asks his brown eyes, searching mine for some sign that I had heard their discussion.

"Oh yeah. But now I need to pee so I can start cleaning up and get ready," I yawn, looking at my watch. I climb from the pile and dart into the restroom, relieving myself before looking into the mirror and letting out a sigh. "Shape up, enjoy what you can and don't be a cry baby," I hiss as I stare into my blue orbs, ordering myself to calm and regain composure.

When I exit into our room, I smile, enjoying the sight of the naked men lounging on the bed where I left them. The bucket still sits next to the fire to keep the water warm, so I hurry over, glancing at my watch again. I grab the wet rag and I wash down my body, grinning around at the very attentive gazes appreciating my slowly drying body.

"Warm towel?" Kent offers as he holds one out.

"Thanks, did I ever receive my rating? Did it stay at amazing?" I ask as I lift an eyebrow and smile.

He grins back, "Fucking mindmelting. Sounds about right."

"I'll take it," I agree with a nod and continue to dry myself off. Reaching for the pile of clothes, Rudolfo moves and hands them to me. "Thanks!" I accept and strap my sister's bra on before I slip into a jet black thong, looking around as the light chatter around me halts. "By your looks, I am bummed that I need to go see Lilly now." Tugging the dress on I yank my fingers through my knotty hair and then twist it up into a bun pausing as I look around for my hair tie.

"Looking for the hair thing?" Nathan asks, sitting up and looking around.

"We have tinsel?" Rudolfo offers as he opens up a drawer to show me the sparkling mess inside. This makes me beam.

With a sigh I bend over, freeing the black thong and using it as a hair tie by twisting it around to ensure that it looks like a lacy scrunchie. I, then, slide my feet into my sister's flats and smoothing the dress down. "*None* of you better let me fall while walking down the aisle. Mr. Campbell might not ever unsee that."

"We can keep you upright for a change. But, no promises after," Mario offers looking at my hair as he nears. His eyes lock on mine, and I want to ask him to make me a deal. I don't, knowing that pushing them wouldn't help anything.

"See you guys out there." I manage, looking up into their faces as they surround me.

"We better look hella good for this pantyless vixen," Nathan beams as he swoops iñ to capture my lips. The others follow suit, leaving me breathless and horny.

A knock at the door helps my distracted mind, and I pull from the quad to open the door before slipping out. Lily shrieks and tugs me through the chilly hall.

Part Five

The wedding goes off without a hitch. Lily finally says 'I do' to Jameson and they are introduced as Mr. and Mrs. Cringle!. The guys and I cheer loud enough for Lilly not to worry about anyone else not being there. The music kicks on and I thank my lucky stars it's not holiday pop. Immediately my hips start swaying and the warm room is filled with laughter and bodies. I take turns dancing with the guys, a few times with two at a time. The heat makes me sweat but the atmosphere is so jubilee that all I can do is smile.

"Shouldn't you pick one already?" Jameson asks, while Lilly fusses with her phone to another playlist she had created.

"Nope, I let Lilly pick the tunes, I don't think she would have let me if I tried," I laugh, swigging back some water and watching Mario's heated gaze on the other side of the fire.

"No Kenna, I mean the guys," Jameson argues, causing my attention to snap to him.

"Excuse me?" I ask frowning. I force myself to cross my arms to remind myself not to punch my brother-in-law.

"Look, I have seen the chemistry but this isn't like one of your slutty books, Kenna. These are my best friends. They don't need games," Jameson says, then gets quiet as someone stops behind me.

"One, I can and will do whoever I want. It's none of your business who I flirt with, sleep with, or look at," I lecture, my tone causing Lilly to pause and the guys to halt in their discussions. "Let it go," I warn, turning to find Mario standing right behind me.

"No, Kenna. You're my family, even before tonight. You have to decide what you want, not just be throwing yourself at all these guys leading them on," Jameson sighs, frowning at Lilly who signals for him to shut up.

"Are you slut shaming me Jameson Cringle?" I ask, letting the acid fill my voice as I watch his face drain of color. My hands drop and I give him my full attention.

"Of course not, I am just looking out for you and my friends…"

"Then stay out of it," Mario suggests, causing me to look up at him.

"Your friends are fine. I am epic and my slutty books hold real life living situations that *you* might not be able to wrap your vanilla mind around but are valid relationships. It's not up to you to decide what I need to do. Or how you think I need to act. They are big boys they can speak for themselves." My lecture ends and Jameson looks over to the guys behind me who whisper to each other.

"Who is that?" Lilly asks, pausing the music that has just started and looking toward the front door. Mr. Campbell rushes over and Jameson moves over to Lilly who begins to quietly berate his behavior.

"Kenna," Mario says, from behind me.

I turn smiling up at him. "That sounded weird." I laugh, "How can I help you Mario?" I ask cheekily.

"Jameson shouldn't talk to you like that," He sighs, looking over at his friend with unveiled anger.

I shrug. "Not worried about it, people can think whatever they want. I know who I am and what I want."

"But we don't want this for you… Look, we had a talk and this thing won't…"

"Santa!" I blurt out, causing him to clamp his mouth shut. I spin around refusing to let the tears burst from my eyes. Why can't I just have the full 24 hours? They had been on the fence. I knew that, but this was too soon.

"I am looking for the officer that has their cruiser up the road." A man dressed in a heavy coat that reads "Police" announces, stomping snow from his boots and looking behind me at the formidable men, assuming it's one of them.

"That would be me, Officer Mckenna Claus. How can I help you?" I ask moving away from Mario and toward the man whose face looks chapped by the cold.

"We have a big mess on our hands, and after getting your car unstuck, we were hoping you would help us to get stranded citizens to the high school until power is restored to all areas?" He asks.

"Let me go change. I'll do what I can to help," I agree, turning not looking at the men who want to reject me and make my way to their room. I lay up quickly, pausing at the desk and snatching on the pen.

My not so Fated Mates,

Thank you for the most amazing Christmas I have ever had. For keeping me warm and satisfied. I hope you all know that I will never forget the experiences I have had this weekend, the fantasies that I thought would never be fulfilled. I hope that someday I find a connection like this again, one that can handle the eyes of the world.

Your Omega

I want to add that I could have been it for them, that I am worth the looks, the chatter. But I refuse to beg, to be petty. They weren't ready and I should respect that. After all, it's not just me that would be under scrutiny.

Once I have everything, I holster my weapon and pocket my phone making sure I have my keys and badge before heading back into the main room. The guys immediately step toward me, but I can't let them finish breaking me. Not when I need to be present and helpful to the world.

"Lilly!" A scream pierces the air and Izzy bounds across the room throwing her snow covered self at my sister. Three more shivering women join her and Jameson starts introducing the girls to my guys. I mean to the guys.

My boots stomp a little harder as I pass Lily and move toward the officer. "You'll need a heavier coat. We have some at the station. We'll take the snowmobiles back out."

"Are you leaving?" Lilly asks, grasping my arms.

"The town needs help. You're fine, your friends are here," I soothe looking at her wide worried eyes.

"You're coming back though, right? Don't let Jameson run you off. I'll talk to him." Lilly hisses at me looking toward the girls who are already flirting with the guys.

"I don't know Lilly. They are not ready to share. Not with the world, at least. I can't live in the shadows, you know that. I'll let you know," I sigh as tears well up in her eyes.

"Thanks again for the ride guys." A male voice booms from near the front door, causing Lilly's face to light up.

"Kenna, that ass is looking so fine. Like always." Lilly's ex, Kyle, greets as his hand slaps my ass when he reaches me.

All the sadness and rage explodes from my body. Kyle cries out as my fist slams into his face and my boot connects with his leg. "Touch me again and I am shooting your balls off. The only reason they aren't splatter now is because I respect Mr. Campbell to much to ruin his property value," I yell as my rage dissipates slightly when all four of the men, that I need with my entire body, approach– their faces filled with a mixture of shock and anger.

"Lilly, your ex is trash stop being his friend already," I growl at my sister whose lips make the perfect 'O' of surprise as she stares down at Kyle on the floor.

"What the actual fuck, Kenna? Do you have to be such a freaking prude?" Kyle whines. clutching his face.

"Is that necessary Kenna? You're going to have to get over this affection aversion one of these days. He was only complimenting you," Izzy lectures in her form of greeting, rushing to help Kyle up from the floor.

"My body, my choice," I growl in reminder as I glance at the guys before making an abrupt about face. I find myself stepping out into the winter wonderland that had literally just yesterday tried to murder me. All the reasons not to leave rush in my ears, but my boots crunch in the snow. I continue forward, choosing to ignore the chaos of my mind. I board the snowmobile, sitting behind one of the police deputies.

I am driven back to my car, where it's been dug out halfway, probably looking for my dead body. After some elbow grease and salts, we have the car back on the road and head to the station, following the snowmobiles carefully down the winding road.

After escorting family after family to the highschool, the dark frozen night sky twinkles down at me as I shake hands with the sheriff and cuddle into my new jacket. I get back into my car, which had been fully gassed up as a thanks for my help, and head back up to the hotel. I want to talk things out with the guys. It wasn't fair for me to leave how I did after shutting them down and giving up on a discussion. When I arrive, I see that the plow had finally made it all the way up the long drive and I park, texting Lilly that I am back and going to chat with the guys. I scroll through the pictures she sent me from the reception, me dancing with them. The passion I feel from them is in those pictures, it's not possible that I am imagining it. I had to fix this. My phone's clock read 2:00 am but it's not like they wouldn't accept me to chat. If they held their ground, I could always head back to town, or even to the next town over, and camp out until I'm up to driving home.

I push open the door, relieved when I don't have to knock, assuming all the girls would be sleeping on the plush couches around the fire. When I near the fire I pause only seeing Kyle, who rolls over and looks up at me in surprise.

"You missed all the fun, as usual," he announces with a stretch and a yawn.

"Where are the girls?" I ask with a frown.

He looks shocked that there is no hostility in my voice and sits up. "Probably still trying to climb the groomsmen like palm trees. They are probably warm and cozy. Need me to warm you up?" Kyle asks with a grin, opening his arms up.

I rest my hand on my gun looking toward the hall to their room. "Thanks for the information." Tears burn at my eyes but I hold back the soul crushing gasps of sadness as I make my way back out of the hotel and to my car. The freezing air battles the hot tears on my face as they stream down but I crank the music, giving no fucks who hears. I drive slowly as I make my way back toward town, making a last minute decision to continue driving until I reach the next one. I need to hide, to lock myself away, and just not exist for a while. After texting Lilly that work came up, I lock the hotel room door and crash onto the bed, the waterfall of emotions pummeling me.

Three days later, I check out of the hotel, the deep circles under my eyes and slight puff to my cheeks going unnoticed by the strangers of this small town. I stop at a gas station, stock up with snacks, this time keeping to myself. The trip home is long and grueling, my phone rings several times but I don't answer it. I eventually text Lilly back telling her that, yes I know we have plans for New Years, and yes, I'll be off work and at home to greet her.

My first stop when I make it back to the city is to check in at work. They still have me out on vacation, and refuse to let me tag in to help or support. If I wasn't so damn sad, I would appreciate them trying. While I'm there, I take a shower, hoping someone will change their mind. Once out, I change into my backup clothes from my locker.

Going home feels like defeat, all that's waiting for me are the reminders that I live in a building alone, now that everyone else on my floor has moved out. Before stopping, I pull in at the store and grab food for tomorrow. I made my sister a promise, and above all else, I had to pull my shit together for her. While at the store, I check my messages from Lilly and listen as she complains that I didn't stay. Talking about how I am missing out on how nice the lodge is with power on. This makes me pause, I hit info and realize that the messages were from an hour or so after I had originally left. When I had gone back, the power had been on. How had I not noticed the outside lights?

I look at her texts, going through the pictures that hurt my heart. As I scroll, I pause at one I never made it to. One of all four girls laying with blankets all over the floor of the chapel, the heading reads Black Mail. *They slept in the chapel?* I wonder, looking at the time stamp that read 6:00 am Dec 26th. Had they been in there when I went back?

Maybe my sister could help clear things up tomorrow. Maybe Jameson would let me have one of their phone numbers so I could explain my thoughts. It wasn't likely, but the hope was what I needed to get me through the store and onto checking my messages. The last of which is from this morning from my building super letting me know that all the rooms on my floor had finally been rented out. A doctor, photographer, lineman, and software developer whom I should make my presence felt so they would feel safe and stay awhile.

I finally found a real reason to go home, get ready for Lilly, and welcome my new neighbors. Some of the weight was finally off my shoulders, and I could feel hope as it began to glimmer deep in my belly. Maybe, just maybe I could talk to them. I let myself into the building, laden down with bags. I take the elevator up to the top–floor seven– and make my way to my door, the sound of music cutting off from two doors down. A door opens behind me as I set a few bags down to unlock my door, making sure none of the wine bottles can fall.

"Omega?" A voice comes from behind me. Heat fills my veins, the bags in my arms crash to the floor. I turn to see them standing across the hall Mario smiling at me with slight worry in his eyes.

"Mine?" I ask, holding myself back as I look into each pair of eyes I have been dreaming of.

"Yours as long as you'll have us," they answer.

My boots thunder across the hall and arms yank me into bear hugs, the breath whooshing from my body, as tears being tears seeping from my eyes. Warmth fills me. They are mine. For a beat, it's safe and consoling. Then, the heat builds in my center. They are mine, for as long as I want. Even if that means I want them forever.

The End

ABOUT THE AUTHOR

B.E.Fidler is the mother of four, currently residing in the Midwest. She began to write after the death of her late stepfather in 1999. Fidler has 35 books in process and enjoys what she calls chaotic writing. Music cranked up, singing at the top of her voice and typing for hours on end. She enjoys writing retreats with her author friends and

Researching her books and practicing the skills her characters utilize on their adventures.

This action-adventure writer strives to bring out readers' emotions in every book she writes.

ALSO, BY B.E. FIDLER ON AMAZON

Catastrophe

The Little Things

The Abominable Things

The Torrential Things

The Contracted Things